Paradise Publishing, LLC
5306 Claymore Meadow Lane
Spring, TX 77389
www.ParadisePublishingHouse.com

Perfect Binding -- 978-1-941680-05-6
Andria Flores, 1974
      1. Perfectionism (Personality trait). 2. Perfectionism—Religious aspects—Christianity. 3. Alcoholics—Family relationships. 4. Memoir—United States.

p. 193
ISBN 978-1-941680-05-6

SUMMARY: Inspired to excel since childhood, a young Christian wife and mother confronts the fallacies of perfectionism when a family secret erodes, and then implodes, her idealized concept of success. Dewey: 248.8

Cover Design by Jen Aiken (jen@jvodesign.com)
Cover Photo © Veou / Adobe Stock
Author Photos by Christopher Cook (PushingTheLens.com)

The paper used in this publication meets the requirements of the American National Standard for Permanence of Paper for Printed Library Materials
Z39.48-1984.First edition.
Printed in the United States of America.

type A plans B

Andria Flores

type A plans B

Andria Flores

Paradise Publishing
Spring, Texas
2020

Dedication

For Mrs. Stroud

You knew since the fourth grade
that there was more to me than
"exceptional wife and mother."
Now I do too.

And for Momma

Thank you for believing in me
when my life became unbelievable.
Thank you for your notebook paper
"text messages" on my windshield.
Thank you for telling me wholeheartedly,
"I can't wait to turn the page."
Above all, thank you for being with me in spirit,
even after you've unexpectedly gone.
I love you as only a daughter can.

Acknowledgements

Dr. Roger Leslie

You are more than a writing coach, editor, and publishing partner. You are a dream. You have singularly made the most significant impact on the content of this book, and consequently left an indelible mark on my heart as I contemplated what all of this meant. I thank God for the day I met you in Denton, Texas, having no idea that you would become a close friend, confidant, mentor, and spiritual guide. I love you, friend.

Jen Aiken

"Just start." Your practical encouragement was just the nudge I needed to set my dreams into motion. I couldn't argue with your logic. Thank you for your sound advice and friendship over countless coffees and grilled shrimp tacos all these years. I am grateful to know you as both a friend and colleague.

My Village

Thank you to all of the women in my life who have picked up one of my children from school, had them stay overnight on short notice, given them a word of encouragement at a game, or an extra hug in the school hallway. I wouldn't know where to begin to thank all of my mom-friends who have helped this single momma juggle daily tasks when life stretched me too thin. You ladies have shown me that there is strength in numbers—and grace in vulnerability.

My Girlfriends

To my closest girlfriends, past and present, thank you for demonstrating that being authentic is endearing and for giving me a safe place to test that theory when it was brand-new and scary. Thank you for being my safety net and loving me for exactly who I am. I will treasure our friendships forever.

My Children

You are pieces of my heart walking around outside of my chest. Thank you for trusting me when you hurt, when you are uncertain, and when I am leading us into something new. Thank you for always believing in me. Son, thank you for genuinely asking me, "How was your day?" then truly listening to my response. And daughter, thank you for every one of your love notes, I'm-really-sorry notes, and I-want-to-be-just-like-you notes. You two make me a better woman.

My Husband

You, my love, are an unexpected gift. You have added so much laughter and peace and safety to my life. You have shown me that real love isn't just for the movies, as I once supposed. Thank you for the respect and dignity you offer in treating me like a partner, not like a princess. Your constant support and unwavering faith frees me to go be awesome, even when that means failing first. I love you with my whole heart—and all the feeeeelings.

Contents

Introduction

My name is Andria Flores, and I have a Type A personality.

I am a classic over-achiever. I grew up in the 80s in a blended family of seven, which made for a long kitchen table in a small breakfast nook, where five kids mocked the outdated wallpaper plastered with large brown and gold-tone fruits and vegetables. My stepmom never liked it either, but I guess between their two full-time jobs, Dad's additional part-times, and their gig as chauffeurs to five kids, little time or inspiration remained for interior design. Maybe that's why Daddy dedicated an entire wall in the kitchen to all of our awards and ribbons, though I just believed it was because we were awesome; it felt like family. Scotch tape and staples affixed our flimsy little grade school awards on top of faded produce, many of them with our names handwritten in Marks-A-Lot with scratch-and-sniff stickers or gold stars in the corners. I was recognized for perfect attendance and making the A Honor Roll. I earned blue and red ribbons for placing in the Science Fair, and green and gold ones for three-legged races and hundred-yard dashes. I was personally driven to earn every gold star I could attain to make my parents proud. In my eyes, any small accomplishment on that wall added value to who I was as a young girl. Every paper award or verbal affirmation, every A+ in red or ribbon in blue validated my significance. It proved I was worthy of love. I worked hard to be the best at anything I ever tried. I was compelled to out-do myself, always raising the bar higher and higher, until eventually, anything less than perfection meant failure to me.

I'm a typical first-born. I was in the first grade when my dad remarried, which demoted me from first-born status to second in line behind my older stepbrother, but not before I had fully mastered the traits of a first-born child. Dr. Kevin Leman nailed it in *The Birth Order Book* describing firstborns as "perfectionistic, reliable, list makers, well-organized, serious, scholarly, natural leaders, self-sacrificing, conservative, supporters of law and order, and self-reliant."[i] Yep, that's me. Bossy big sister. First Chair French Horn. President, Treasurer, or Secretary of nearly every organization I ever joined. I rarely said no to an opportunity to be in charge or to organize something, and adulthood didn't slow me down. I was Sunday School Teacher, Room Mom, Youth Pastor…the numbered list goes on. Leading and serving others gave me a sense of fulfillment—and doing it "perfectly," a sense of self-worth. Perfectionism and leadership were mine by nature. These roles were modeled for me at home as well, until ultimately they defined me.

I'm a super-hero's daughter. Through my little girl eyes, my daddy did everything right. Daddy is a good Southern man, a retired firefighter, and a mechanic. Not only was he a public servant, but I witnessed his private service to others my whole life as well. I've seen him repair numerous cars at no charge for family and friends. Road trips were commonly diverted when he stopped to aid a stranded motorist, or boating trips curtailed so he could tow in a disabled boater. As a child, I put him on a pedestal, and he put me on one as well. He seemed to think I could do no wrong, and I rarely tested that theory. To me, Daddy was perfect, and I soaked it all in. From the explicit instructions he gave for folding washcloths, to his rigid expectations for spotless rooms, clean closets and sock drawers, to his dogged determination to read the instruction manual for every single piece of equipment our family ever owned before we could even take it out of the box, Daddy did things right. He expected no less from us. Without question, I lived to please that man. I'm all grown up now so I know better, but as a child I believed my dad was flawless, and I internalized the hell out of that.

I might be a little OCD, though I prefer the term *highly organized*. I like right angles and straight lines. My stapler and tape dispenser are uniformly aligned on my desk, as they should be. My pantry looks more like a grocery store aisle with all the cans and packages in perfect rows, labels facing forward. I have been known to straighten a water bottle or two in the convenience store refrigerated section. I'm sure I need some sort of therapy for this. But actually, I consider the perpetual straightening my own form of therapy. If my bed is crisply made and my canned goods face front, then I can mentally afford to let my daughter wear shorts and two different colored knee socks out of the house. If my office supplies are in perfect alignment, I can leave my son to his own meticulous system of sorting Legos into a dozen brown paper Starbucks sacks, rather than organizing them in clear plastic totes like any sane person would do. As a matter of fact, this is precisely how we maintain some sense of sanity at our house. I control the things that matter to me and to no one else, so I am rarely compelled to control anyone else, their Legos, or their socks.

I am a recovering perfectionist.

I like to be right. If I'm not absolutely certain I'm right, I like to be quiet and invisible. I'm either the kid whose hand shoots up first with the *Ooo! Oooo! Ooooo!* Or, I'm the one who's instantly analyzing carpet fibers in a desperate attempt to avoid any eye contact whatsoever. In school, I was the girl whose face turned bright red and whose eyes held back big tears when I was wrong...even over a simple math fact. The driving force hurling me toward perfectionism for four decades of my life has always been fear. Fear of being wrong. Fear of not fitting in. Fear of chopsticks and long division. Fear of misunderstanding, and certainly fear of being misunderstood. I spent most of my life scared of what others would think of me when I didn't get it right. Math facts, life choices, or menu selections: fear paralyzed me, and I didn't even realize it.

Andria Flores

Fear set me up to measure my self-worth by my ability to meet or exceed the expectations of others—or at least what I perceived their expectations to be. As a result, I imposed unreasonable standards on myself. I believed I was always under a microscope, when in truth no one was even looking at me. The only person obsessing over my failures and successes was me. Still I kept chasing impossible ideals in order to please others and bolster my own self-worth. Until my mid-thirties, I had no idea how much value I gave to what I perceived others thought of me. It just seemed natural to constantly question myself. The doubts ran swiftly through my head like the ticker on CNN: *What if I am not smart enough? Not pretty enough? Not talented enough? Not quiet enough? Not serious enough?* Not good enough.

Obsessed with garnering approval, I fixated on my ability to perform. Particularly during my formative years, my focus on identifying and fulfilling what I believed others expected of me left me little time to consider what I expected of myself. As a result, I failed to develop my own dreams. Other than being an exceptional wife and mother, which I had firmly set my heart on in the fourth grade, I never settled on what I wanted to be when I grew up. I just kept chasing others' expectations, which caused me to gravitate toward people who needed me.

Three decades later, I was married with two children, and I cherished my roles in their lives. I was deeply fulfilled as a wife and a mother. Perfectionism and people-pleasing had worked nicely for me to that point. That lifestyle won me everything I imagined for myself—and for all the world to see—a perfect life with a doting husband and two delightful children. Board by board, I had successfully constructed my white picket fence. It wasn't intentional, rather the result of one perfect choice after another.

By my mid-thirties however, the fence was beginning to splinter. I slowly awakened to the fact that I didn't know who I was, what I liked, or what I was good at on my own. I was beginning to realize that nearly every success in my life was directly related to the success of someone else, particularly my husband and my children. William successfully grew his accounting business while I stayed home to raise our children and offer him administrative and marketing support. We built a beautiful home; we had two children, a daughter and a son; and we actively engaged ourselves in church. But when life got rocky, I was at a loss for how to deal with it, so I pretended everything was still perfect.

I was unprepared for imperfection and failure.

My marriage was deteriorating, but no one knew because I discreetly hid our problems behind my pristine little fence. My husband was slipping away from us one margarita at a time. My toddler was developing an independent little personality of her own that did not lend itself well to Mommy's perfectionism. My infant son struggled to breastfeed, so after only three months I quit, which led me to blame myself relentlessly for his minor health issues that followed. Outside of our home, I longed for more connection in my relationships, but I couldn't let people in past the gate. My lifelong relationship with God was beginning to feel rigid and religious, like going through the Bible-reading-church-going motions. I craved authenticity. But I didn't know how to do authenticity without revealing all of my flaws and failures. So a whole new set of doubts raced through my mind: *What if I've wrecked my son's immune system? How does someone as rigid as me raise an outspoken, free-spirited daughter? How do I cope with my husband's alcoholism? How the hell do I get real AND keep this white picket fence from falling down around me?*

I was not equipped to deal with imperfection or failure. Yet it was piling on faster than I could handle. I read any resource promising to solve it. I devoured popular parenting books and determined to become a better mother to my daughter and son. I stood in resolute faith for my husband and our marriage. I prayed for strength, for peace, and for change. I quoted scriptures, wrote them in my journals, and taped them to my bathroom mirror. I attended Bible studies where I genuinely sought God and began opening myself up just a little to other women of faith. For nearly seven years, I worked my ass off to fix everything that no one even knew was broken. Just like the nine-year-old me counting awards on the kitchen wall, I set out to be the best I could possibly be. I just knew if I tried hard enough, I could win approval and love. I could perfect my way through my problems, and no one would have to know anything was ever wrong.

But I failed.

Being perfect finally wore too thin. Perfectionism could no longer sustain the life I had set out to live. I wanted to be real more than I wanted to be right.

CHAPTER 1

A Type A Perfectionist

Brown paper sacks

I panicked when I noticed the brown paper sack in plain view on top of the bar in our kitchen. A couple from our church stopped by to drop off their tax work to my husband, William. The four of us had just sat down in the living room when I realized it was still sitting there staunchly open. I popped up off the couch to make myself busy in the kitchen while the three of them continued chatting in the living room. I smiled and laughed as a part of their conversation, but my heart raced as I pretended to putter around the kitchen and discreetly move the sack out of sight. *Did they already see it? Could they tell it's from the liquor store? Oh my God...* I silently panicked.

Drinking was forbidden in the church and ministry in which we were involved. I habitually hid the evidence. I shoved empty bottles deep into our trashcan. I cushioned them so they wouldn't clank together on the street on trash day, but that never muffled the sounds when the trash men hurled our bags into their truck. I folded brown paper sacks in such a way that the words "Majestic Liquor Store" wouldn't show. The sheer number of paper sacks I tucked away each week was indication enough that my husband had a problem. Every morning, I wiped down sticky counter tops and tile floors where William mixed his drinks the night before. I got on my hands and knees to fervently scrub purple drops and sloshes out of our creamy white carpet after the occasional wine nights. The worst were the syrupy spills dripping into the cushions of our leather reclining sofa where he sat nightly in front of the TV with his margaritas. Those were the hardest to clean, and the most frequent. I kicked the recliner back and rubbed a warm washcloth and mild soap between the seats almost daily as I picked up his gummy glass, only an inch of a watered down cocktail remaining from the ice that had melted overnight.

The warmth of the washcloth brought the sour smells to life. I hated the smells. The air was laden with fermented alcohol at 9:00 in the morning where he laid in our bedroom, still sleeping when I walked back in after dropping our children to elementary school and pre-school. The musty stench engulfed me when I entered his upstairs office, whether he was in there or not. On Sunday mornings, beneath his cotton undershirt and crisp white button-down and tie, through the layers of his expensive suit, I could smell the pungent, stale odor on his skin. It's not the fresh aroma of salt and limes and the sweetness of tequila that reveals an alcoholic. It's the acidic, rancid emanation seeping from the pores of a man who has soaked himself in alcohol from the inside out.

I was ashamed to sit next to him on the pew that way, and my shame made me feel like a horrible wife. I felt so guilty for the lack of respect that was growing inside of me for my husband. I wanted to revere him, but God, it was getting harder to do. I struggled with what that must mean about me as a Christian wife. I despaired over what that surely revealed about my faith. Nevertheless, daily he was desperate to drink, and I was obsessive about covering it up. It became a waltz. He made drinks, and spilled, and slept it off. I disposed of bottles, scrubbed stains, and tidied up…and I hid brown paper sacks.

Fourth grade ideals

Ours was not the ideal marriage I had dreamed of in the fourth grade. It had been, once. So I'm not entirely sure how we landed there. Addiction was certainly never part of my plan. When I was nine years old, my Type A personality was already in full swing with checklists and plans for becoming an ideal wife and a mother *and* an astronaut. I had everything all laid out, and not once was there room for something like alcoholism—or any problem, really.

My husband and I were happy for years. We began with nothing. Sometimes we counted up all our quarters so we could go to Sonic for cheeseburgers. We didn't mind. We were just starting out in our meager little apartment in a small town just outside of Fort Worth, Texas. We worked in ministry together and went to church together. We developed careers—he in accounting, and I in business administration. William worked for various businesses and organizations doing accounting and tax work with the goal of having his own full-time firm. Personally and professionally, I gravitated toward supporting others, which made me an attentive and thorough executive assistant. I excelled in any position I took, and I began making good money in my field. He did well also, so it wasn't long until we wore nice clothes, bought new cars, and built a beautiful home in a reputable school district. We had babies—first Reese, then James. We regularly volunteered to teach children's classes at church and over the years became youth pastors. We were happy doing all of the things we felt made us a solid, contributing couple.

The pinnacle for me was being able to come home just prior to our daughter's birth and fulfill my dreams of becoming a stay-at-home wife and mother. By her first birthday, William came home as well to manage his accounting and tax firm full-time from our home office, and I assisted him as needed. I built relationships with clients, entered receipts and balanced bank accounts, developed his online presence, and networked with local business owners in a nearby town—*and* I got to

Andria Flores

be wife and momma! We were living the perfect life I had imagined for myself. But something changed.

A perfect life, interrupted

We took a trip to Cancun to celebrate our sixth wedding anniversary. Just for fun, we decided to have strawberry daiquiris at a quaint little patio restaurant in Mexico. And that decision altered our lives forever. The daiquiri was wonderful —so sweet and cold and bursting with strawberry flavor. I could feel its warm buzz in my head almost immediately. That velvety red drink was such a treat to me! I was too naïve to realize how dangerous it was for him. Within weeks after we retuned home from our trip, he had already formed a habit, drinking alone several nights a week.

I don't even know what triggered William's drinking problem. I'm such an over-thinker, I should have figured it out, but honestly I have never felt conclusive about it. I have theories, of course. But they are only my personal subjections about what may have made him feel sad, oppressed, or defeated, or simply what may have ignited his dormant addiction to alcohol from his early twenties. Regardless of the intricacies of physiology and addiction, the fact remained that he was drinking heavily.

In the same weeks that followed our vacation, I discovered I was pregnant with our second child. We wanted to have our children close together, so I was elated that they would be just fifteen months apart. I wanted them to be close like my little brother and I were. William and I were even happier as the months passed and we found out we were having a boy! One of each. Perfect.

However, six months into my pregnancy, he drank excessively—daily. He started just before dinnertime and drank until he passed out close to midnight. As thrilled as I was about our second child on the way, my heart grew heavy as I watched my husband drink himself away from us nightly. When he drank, he got quiet and distant. His eyes became glassy, and I knew he was somewhere else. Losing my husband to alcohol every night broke my heart as a woman, and it increasingly threatened my dream of a perfect life as a wife and mother. My concerns for our family were growing faster than my belly, and my awareness of my dependence on him was beginning to tighten around my throat. His drinking affected his business. I worried that I needed to go back to work. But who would hire someone six months pregnant, knowing that she would be on maternity leave in a matter of weeks? It's not what I wanted in my heart, but I approached William to see what he thought about me looking for some extra work so I could help contribute to our income again. He laughed and grinned, "You aren't nearly as independent as you think you are. I've got everything under control." I felt small and fenced in.

One evening while our daughter spent the night with my mom, I shimmied my round belly behind the wheel of my car and took a long drive on a straight road I knew toward Granbury. I cried hard. I got all the way to the edge of that little town, and I turned back around. I feared that if I drove any farther past this road I knew, I might just fall off the map. I wasn't driving to leave my husband; I was driving to figure out how to save my marriage. I needed to think. *Is my husband really an alcoholic? Surely, he will get this fixed. What if he doesn't? What will this do to our marriage?* These were the most ominous dilemmas I had ever faced in my life, and I had no idea how to fix them. I felt frozen—paralyzed and numb.

Living a double life

We continued to serve at church. William volunteered us for positions that he felt gave us status. We shouldn't have been serving in ministry at that point at all. It began to feel disingenuous, but just like the empty bottles, I stuffed those feelings down deep because I, too, wanted to hide our problems. I cushioned them with volunteer work, and cleaning, and anything else that would quiet my mind and save me from having to confront them too often. I wanted to protect the life we created, so I hid everything. I covered for him—and for me. I wanted no one to know what was actually going on in our home. So as William continued to volunteer us for more positions at church, I spent Saturday nights preparing Sunday School lessons and weeknights preparing Youth messages. Meanwhile, he drank and slipped away somewhere else in his mind.

I didn't challenge him much. I just got things done. I kept up appearances for the both of us. I don't think I believed it was really going to be a long-term problem. I thought that since he knew in his own heart that he wasn't making good choices, he would pull himself out of it. Giving him time and space to manage or overcome his addiction didn't help him though. It made things worse. Without personal strength or accountability, William sank deeper into his addiction to alcohol, and I clung tighter to my addiction to perfection. We upheld the image of who we genuinely once were, only now we were living a lie.

When Reese was two years old and James about four months, we decided to take a summer vacation to San Antonio to visit Sea World. It was about a five-hour drive from our home in Fort Worth. We left late one afternoon thinking the kids might sleep in the car after we stopped for dinner. They didn't, and naturally they became fussy. Because it was the time of day he normally began drinking, William's patience grew very thin as he drove us south on I-35 approaching Waco.

He began snapping at me to control the kids. I climbed into the backseat as we sped down the highway. No one said it, but we both knew he needed a drink. We ended up picking up beer at a gas station and getting a hotel less than two hours from home. I hated that trip. I felt so much shame that he was drinking, that I couldn't keep the kids from fussing, and that we weren't having a picture perfect family vacation.

The one thing I cherished about that trip was watching our daughter's eyes light up at Sea World during the dolphins and acrobatics show. It was absolutely mesmerizing to her, and the awe on her hot, flushed countenance was pure bliss for me. I closed my eyes and memorized her face in my heart. I relished holding our infant son while he drank from a bottle and napped against my skin, despite sweating in the insanely humid San Antonio heat. I adored pushing James contentedly in his stroller and misting him with a spray bottle of water as the pediatrician recommended so he wouldn't overheat. Those are the stories and photos I shared with friends and family when we returned, not the extra night at a hotel, or climbing into the backseat, or beer at a gas station.

"I have it under control."

I tried to confront William about his drinking once, early on—that first year, perhaps. I was beyond the comfort of my gentle temperament and passive tone with him. Seeing all the bottles stashed in the freezer and hidden in the pantry finally sent me over the top.

When he sauntered into the kitchen late one morning for more coffee, I opened the doors to the pantry and the freezer and insisted, "You need to get this out of our house. Today."

He stared at me blankly.

I remained calm, but stern, making it a random and awkward stand I took with him, "Do you understand what I am saying? I don't want to see these bottles in my freezer or pantry anymore. Get them out today, please."

He became condescending and literal, as he rolled his eyes and walked off toward the garage. He grabbed an empty liquor box and came back to the kitchen. He carefully packed up the bottles between the cardboard inserts, and carried them "out of the house" and into the garage.

He sneered back at me, "I'll take care of it—but, *you* need to be careful how you speak to me."

I instantly felt small again. My attempt at assertiveness only made him angry and left me in tears. Clearly, I had no control. Instead, we slipped back into our predictable pattern of drinking, cleaning, and covering. We did this dance for years. Eventually, I seldom talked to him about it anymore. I might casually mention it to him every few months, but not with the conviction and directness I had that one afternoon.

I believe William and I were good people, just broken. I dealt with broken the only way I knew how: hide it and fix it, then sneak it back in when no one was looking. I prayed on my knees, lifted my hands, leaned on my faith, and stood on scripture. I did all the things I was taught to do in church, without actually revealing to anyone in church what we were going through. I felt stuck in this cycle…and weary. I was running out of ideas and faith projects to fix us. I continued to believe that if I covered for him, it would buy him time to get himself together, and no one would ever have to know about our mess behind closed doors.

Andria Flores

William would promise, "I have it under control." He would profess, "I'll quit on Monday." Or, "This time will be different." But after seven years of unfulfilled words, I was losing faith in him, and it killed me. I was worn out from hiding and keeping secrets. At church or with friends, my face burned red because of the sour smells of alcohol on his skin, and almost constantly now my heart burned for allowing myself to feel the sting of his broken promises over and over again. It took me nearly seven years of ardently, but quietly, fighting for our marriage, before I dared to speak out with conviction against his drinking again.

The day I yelled at him

One morning he was traveling to East Texas to see a tax client, and I called him about some little thing regarding our children. It was trivial, but I was so emotionally overwhelmed from the stress of his drinking and my pretending that I ended up crying uncontrollably over the phone. Initially, I despised myself for losing control of my emotions. But then, my desperation gave way to anger, and with all of that momentum behind me I raised my voice.

"I can't take it anymore! Your drinking is ruining our marriage! I can't keep carrying it all by myself."

He remained silent on the other end of the line, maybe because he was in shock that I had raised my voice, or maybe because I didn't even pause to take a breath.

Adrenaline added fuel to my bottled emotions, and I was suddenly lit. I recounted to William how heavy his addiction had become to me, "I can't keep hiding and pretending everything is so perfect. It hurts. I HURT!" Then I grew louder still, "You have to do something! I can't carry the weight of this anymore!"

I yelled. In our thirteen years of marriage, I rarely ever lost my composure or raised my voice. I was entirely too buttoned-up to holler and too scared of disapproval to say how I really felt. Once I started though, I kept shouting into the phone through broken sobs, "I can't carry this anymore! It's too heavy! YOU do something! YOU fix this!"

My tank finally empty, I drew a breath.

In the awkward silence that followed, William replied with shortness in his tone, "I have a plan to quit."

I was momentarily in shock that he didn't yell back at me.

Then he scolded, "Don't ever talk to me like that again. I know what I'm doing, and I have it under control. Besides, I don't know how this possibly affects you."

I was so relieved to finally be that honest with him—and that he didn't yell back at me—that I silently dismissed the last few things he said to me. I told myself, *He just doesn't understand. But none of that matters if he plans to quit drinking.*

I genuinely thought things would change. So, I spent the whole day tidying up the house, making sure the children were well-rested, picking up their toddler toys, and alternating ice packs and cold cream on my puffy eyes. I fed the kids an early dinner. Then, I showered and slipped on something fresh and feminine. With a hopeful heart, I anticipated his return that evening and the two of us making time to talk about a clean start.

When he arrived home, he went straight to the kitchen and mixed himself a margarita. Stunned, I shrank back into the little person I actually felt like, not the woman who spoke her mind nine hours earlier. He sat down in front of the TV with his drink, and I made myself busy with dishes and bedtime routines. I said nothing.

Four fragile words

A few weeks later I mustered the courage to confront him once more. This time I took a different approach: my calm, steady, emotionally-controlled demeanor he had always praised me for. I gathered my thoughts in advance, took Reese and James to Mom's for the night, and I asked William if we could talk. I sat across from my husband at our dining room table, and I shared my heart, something I rarely took the risk to do with anyone. I calmly expressed to him that something had to change, that I was willing to do anything we needed to do to get him help, but I couldn't go on like this. Completely depleted in every sense, I let him know I was even considering divorce. He responded that he would handle it.

Neither of us ever called *it* by its actual name: alcoholism. We referred to his drinking problem as *it*. He would handle *it*. He had *it* under control. I would pray about *it*. That night, after I vulnerably opened myself up to my husband in our dining room, my heart racing at my own transparency, he promised he would end *it* for good. I believed him because I wanted to. I was desperate to. I got up from the table, sat in William's lap, wrapped my arms around his neck, and allowed tears of relief to fall freely down my cheeks. He gave me a short pat-pat on the shoulder, wiggled himself away, and made himself a drink.

The potential loss of our marriage and family wasn't enough to break his addiction. That's not how that works. I'd like to say I got my thoughts together and created a strategy for my children and myself. But I didn't. Instead, I fell apart. I leaned even harder into my addiction for perfection by frantically hiding, and not just his bottles and paper sacks. I hid my shame. I hid my puffy eyes. I hid my heart.

I don't know why he numbed himself with alcohol all those years, but I numbed too. I numbed my pain with sleep. Sometimes after he got out of bed in the morning, I would give myself an hour to slide back under the covers and cry or close my eyes, while he went upstairs to work. I numbed my shame with pretending. Being a Room Mom in both my children's classrooms gave me the connection I wanted with them now that they were in school. It also became another outlet for my pursuit of perfection. I hid more than candy-filled plastic eggs at class Easter parties; I hid pain, embarrassment, and flaws. It appeared I led the perfect

Andria Flores

life if you measured me by the Pinterest-inspired birthday parties I hosted for my children with birthday cakes I baked myself, but these too were now a departure from our real life. I numbed my worries and fears with dusting and vacuuming. My house was spotless. Always. Appearance was something I could control, and the outward order seemed to mask our inward mess.

I was losing my ability to hold it all together though. Neither an immaculate home, nor homemade bumblebee and Nascar birthday cakes, nor a mild-mannered disposition proved to my husband how wonderful I was. None of these efforts made me more valued or noticed—or loved. In fact, I began to resent his lack of appreciation for all the gestures I was making in our home, at our school, and for our church. *What else could I possibly do to prove my worth to him as a wife and mother? What could I do to make William want us more than he wanted another drink?* After seven long years of trying, I finally grew angry.

One weekend, after another night of his drunkenness and my disappointment, we fought. Not yelling and shouting, just distance and dirty looks from him in the stands at the kids' basketball games and in front of my mother. I could handle it at home, but I despised him for treating me that way in front of other people. Finally, after we got home that evening and the kids had gone away with Mom for the night, a few words from me broke the silent treatment I had received all day. Four hard words from my shaky, fragile voice marked the turning point from dedicating all of my energies to preserving our marriage, to letting it go and preserving a life for myself and my children.

"I want a divorce."

CHAPTER 2

No Plan B

"I want a divorce."

I'm not sure I know exactly what a breakdown looks like because I've always been so emotionally controlled, but that's what it felt like from the moment I spoke those words. In all our years of marriage, William and I had agreed that divorce was off-limits. We never used that word as an option or as a weapon. So I never formed an exit plan, even when it was imminent. But once I said those four words to him, I didn't look back. For me, it was over. I was finally done. That very night, we began sleeping in separate rooms. I struggled to grasp the enormity of what lay ahead. One of my greatest sources of security had always been having a plan, knowing what's next, and being prepared like a Girl Scout. After I turned the corner toward divorce, I had none of these things, and it scared the living hell out of me.

I started doing things I had never done before. I told my parents and closest friends I was leaving. I looked at rental houses, opened new bank accounts, and pondered how to re-enter the workforce after eight years out raising my children. Apart from William now, and having never really made these kinds of decisions on my own, I grappled to understand how to do the simplest things. By the grace of God, I came across the kindest real estate agent, Lisa, as I was looking for a house to rent. I'm sure she didn't earn any kind of commission for her time, but like an angel, she guided me along in the process and showed my mom and me a handful of houses until we found one I wanted to lease in the same town as Mom. Lisa even negotiated with the property manager to lower the monthly rent by fifty dollars.

Dad was emotionally supportive from a distance. He remained even-keeled, which is definitely my dad. His side of our family is very "live and let live," which means we don't get into each other's business. While I was aching for a little of that, I absolutely did not expect it. I felt like an utter failure, so the last thing I wanted to do was ask for help. I felt like I got myself into this mess, and I deserved to bear the burden of getting myself out—shrouded in shame the whole way.

Mom continued to be supportive in practical ways. When moving day arrived, she showed up in front of our pretty suburban two-story home with her horse trailer and a couple of men from her ranch to help load my belongings to move over to my new rental house. It was an awkward scene I would have chuckled about had I not been the one having my nice leather sofa shoved

Andria Flores

onto a dirty old trailer because I was leaving my husband. That's what people saw…me leaving my husband. Hardly anyone knew why. He wasn't telling, and neither was I. The exposure was overwhelming. Ironically, we were still hiding the issues. But you can't very well hide a smelly horse trailer in the middle of your street containing your sofa and mattress while the neighbors come out to see what's going on. The shame and uncertainty were excruciating. I felt like I was burning white hot from the inside out.

My exit from our waltz was anything but graceful. Every single step I took required a concerted effort, like I suddenly had concrete blocks for feet. Still my children and I made it out with an old living room set, a worn mattress and box springs, bunk beds that were given to us, and towels and sheets that had been packed away in the attic for the next garage sale. It was incredibly humbling, not in the sense that I no longer had nice things, rather that I had need. I hated to need. I preferred self-sufficiency and the ability to give to others. I truly enjoyed serving and caring for others; I liked being needed. I was unfamiliar and wildly uncomfortable to be the one in need. I was unprepared for the move, unsure of our next steps, and uncertain of our future as a whole. I needed help.

What the hell?

The first weeks and months the kids and I spent in our new house felt loud and in slow-motion, like the minutes following a car wreck. My ears were ringing with all the undeniable noise in my life, while everything around me felt disorienting and surreal. That's what it was like to pull into a new garage, to toss my keys onto an unfamiliar counter top, or place milk in an empty refrigerator passed on to me from my late grandmother's house. My marriage, my family, my home, my perfect image and plans were all gone. I spent most days feeling raw and in shock. This new, unplanned life was marked with unanswered questions, lots of crying, and painful conversations with my children.

Many of my friends came out of the woodwork to let me know how selfish I was for not standing in faith for my husband. Within the first few days, when I was falling apart and watching everything spin out of control, my heart leapt when my closest friend, Mia, called. I knew that her own life circumstances, and her glimpses into mine, would lend her the understanding I needed about my choice to leave, even if she disagreed. I quickly answered the phone eager for the compassion I craved and anticipated I would hear in her voice. Instead Mia berated me for not being a more patient and supportive wife. She made it clear that I was ruining my children's lives. She advised that I needed to "suck it up" and "be willing to sacrifice" for my husband and for our children. Mia crushed me. So did other women and couple-friends we had. I was so beaten down by my own guilt and shame that I didn't even defend myself to them; neither did I reveal the extent of the problems I had hidden for so

Andria Flores

many years. I just took it all in. I let their words puncture my heart like arrows because I felt I deserved the sting.

The storm that had been brewing and swirling inside our home, undetected from the outside for years, had finally broken loose and decimated our family. The life I had worked so diligently to create, then spent years to protect, was all out in the open now, broken in shambles. The one thing I had set my heart on in life was destroyed, and I had no idea where to go from there. All I could think was, "What the hell?"

I pulled the trigger on divorce. Yet I was just as stunned as everyone else that it was actually happening. In the midst of all the heartache and chaos that ensued, and the total leveling of white picket fences, I found myself completely without a plan. Wracked with pain for myself and—God in Heaven—for my children, I grieved heavily for them and for what they were losing. My tenderhearted little boy in Pre-K, and my spunky, outgoing second grade daughter, were crying tears I couldn't console. Tucking them into their hand-me-down beds at night was the most emotional time of day for all three of us. I couldn't get through it without tears, even when they did.

My babies were robbed of the perfect family I desperately wanted to give them. A large piece of innocence and youth were ripped from Reese and James, and they had no control over it whatsoever. I ached deeply for them. I also mourned the loss of my lifestyle as a wife and mother. It was my lifelong dream, and those roles had ultimately defined me as a person. I had vested all of my worth as a woman into my ability to perform them flawlessly. And here I was, no longer a wife, a newly single mother, and an emotional wreck—completely fumbling through every decision.

"Well, I'll tell you one thing, you're one hell of an actress."

I'll never forget my mother's shock when I told her I was seeking a divorce. She was equally stunned when I disclosed William's alcoholism and what had really been going on in our home for nearly seven years. Mom and I were close, but she had no idea. In retrospect I can imagine it was quite a lot to suddenly take in. Everything seemed perfect until the dam broke. Me—I was the dam. I held back the problems, the tears, and the pain with a concrete wall of perfection. I prevented our flawed life from spilling over and flooding our perfect one. I didn't want anyone, including my own mother, to know we were anything less than the happy couple we had projected ourselves to be. I will never forget what she said to me just a few short weeks after I broke the news to her. I was driving around a corner when she blurted from the passenger seat, "Well, I'll tell you one thing, you're one hell of an actress."

To this day, I can feel the weight of her words on my chest and the electricity that shot through my heart. Momma was right, but I had never seen it. I had been nailed between the eyes with truth. I was one hell of an actress. She kind of chuckled with disbelief when she said it, wide-eyed with surprise. She wasn't disappointed, or angry, or embarrassed of me. She was not shaming me. She was sitting right beside me, literally and emotionally, in complete shock that I had pulled it off. She couldn't believe I had successfully pretended everything was so wonderful, when in fact my marriage had been failing for years. Mom was having a hard time taking in my situation, and with both hands on the wheel, I was having a hard time taking in her words.

An actress? As in a fake? I had never once seen myself that way. I had seen a devoted wife, a nurturing mother, and a Christian woman. At 37 years old, I still felt like a "good girl" trying to do the right thing; hell, still trying to please my parents, my husband, my church, my friends. It never occurred to me that working so damn hard to be perfect had actually made me plastic. Not once had I considered myself to be fake because the desire in my heart to keep our family together was so real. Hiding our problems was never an intentional act of deception. It was a series of acts of desperation. And yet, scene by scene, I had been playing the role of supporting actress in my own life, always the accommodating wife and attentive mother. Momma was right. I was one hell of an actress.

Her words were never intended to hurt. My mother was far and away my biggest supporter during my divorce. She and my stepdad stood by my side until I could stand on my own two feet. But her words cut right through the bullshit. For seven years of our thirteen-year marriage, I had hidden our imperfections exceptionally well. I was one hell of an actress who had never been bold enough to take the lead. Now that I was longing to find my own voice and step out into a new role, all hell was breaking loose, and I was scrambling to formulate Plan B.

Plan B really pisses me off.

Going through a life-changing event like divorce, or death, or terminal illness, can make even the simplest situations feel complex. Something as normal as a friend or acquaintance asking, "How are you doing?" could send my mind reeling. *Have they already heard I'm getting a divorce? Is this small talk? Is it okay to say I'm fine? Should I say I'm a mess, or I'm hurting, or—oh my gosh—am I starting to cry right now?* Yeah, all of that, at once.

It rarely ended well. The truth is after I separated from my ex-husband, that's all I thought about directly or indirectly. My mind was always a thousand miles away, so when someone asked me a simple question like, "How are you doing?" I was at a loss. I finally learned I needed a short answer. Unless it was my mom or a close friend, I needed an answer I could go to in an instant, one that was genuine, but not too revealing. I learned to say, "We're doing well." Or to deflect with, "I'm alright. How are you?" Or, "Today is a good day" …or a hard day. Seemingly simple situations became surreal. Nearly every routine was laced with new feelings, like the first time I went to a parent-teacher conference, or family Christmas, or another child's birthday party, as a divorced parent.

Harsh realities come crashing down on all of us in otherwise moments of normalcy. When a woman loses her husband to death, she can numb her way through the days that follow planning his funeral, standing graveside, and accepting casseroles from well-meaning church families. But when she instinctively reaches for him in the night, reality comes crashing down hard. He's not there. And he's never coming back. The same was true for the kids and me. Moments of normalcy seemed to shake their fists in our faces to remind us of our uncomfortable and painful new reality.

One reality that struck hard for me those first weeks on my own was laundry. I was gathering the kids' dirty clothes one night in our rental house while they were spending the night with their dad. The house was painfully quiet. I missed their constant chatter and non-stop noise. I wanted to make them dinner, put them to bed, and cuddle them up...*normal* mom-stuff. But they were gone. The reality struck that my babies were not underfoot and in my arms, and I couldn't change that.

I dropped a basket full of their dirty clothes right in the middle of the hallway and wept an angry cry. I hit my knees and hugged size six and eight t-shirts to my chest. I inhaled grass stains and strawberry lip-gloss from their tank tops and jeans. I missed them terribly, the kind of missing someone that made a knot in my chest that just wouldn't let go of my heart. It was hard to breathe. I was distraught that Reese and James were not sleeping under the same roof as me. I was left to wash and fold little boy socks and little girl pajamas with no children to put them on. This was not what I had planned for my life—or theirs. **God is a Planner too.**

His words, not mine.

"'For I know the plans I have for you,' says the Lord."

"Well, it's a good thing," I told Him through hot tears, "because I don't."

I cried everywhere now—the hallway, the sofa, the driver's seat, the shower, behind my big dark sunglasses at the soccer field. I didn't know the plans He had for me. I didn't even know the plans I had for myself.

Frequently after I left my ex-husband, I asked God, "What the hell am I going to do now?"

Apparently, He's heard this question before because to my surprise, He answered, "Baby girl, I know the plans I have for you..."[ii]

When God talked to me, I melted. Fear dripped from me like hot wax, thick and slow. In my moments of uncertainty, panic, and the ugly cries, that's all I needed to know. *God has a plan for me.* I breathed in indescribable peace in my darkness, and tiny seeds of faith buried deep in my heart slowly began to germinate. *Faith*, because I didn't know the plan, but God did, and He was speaking to me. He didn't roll out a ten-year strategy with charts and maps and bullet points, as I would have liked. He just gave me His Word that He had a plan. *Faith*, because He was offering nebulous mysteries to me like hope and a future, not the milestones and absolutes that had always proven to be a source of security for me in the past. *Faith*, because all of the anchors in my life were gone: my husband, my home, my close friends, the means to provide for my children, and my plans—even my plans.

Right in the middle of my loudest fears, I let myself feel the whispers of God on my heart. Our little moments of faith were making me curious about trusting Him instead of myself. It wasn't the faith I experienced before, culminating from church attendance, praying scriptures, and reading daily devotionals. It was faith born of relationship, tiny and tender. I began to tentatively share my heart with God, to neglect the pew on Sunday and simply acknowledge His presence in the car, on the carpet, and at the soccer field. I wondered if I could believe in God for myself, and if He might believe in me too.

Leaning into this new faith—even just the slightest bit— demonstrated to me that I could have moments of peace without a map. I was finding courage to navigate with my compass alone, just making sure I was still headed in the right direction, one small step at a time, the girl who doesn't have a plan and the God who does.

CHAPTER 3

Living in Fear, But Calling It Faith

"Do the best you can in the situation you are in."

In between moments of faith, I was forced to do the best I could do in the situation I was in. Growing up, I heard my dad offer that advice countless times. I was used to the mantra, but unfamiliar with the reality of actually implementing it. I was accustomed to playing it safe, not taking risks. I really hadn't been challenged with very many hard things in my life, so I rarely found myself in truly difficult situations where I had to make the best of my circumstances. But leaving my ex-husband—that brought on the most uncertainty and overwhelm I had ever faced, and I was afraid.

In my life so far, playing by the rules and meeting expectations had given me a skewed sense of confidence and control. I was faithful to obey the rules, so I anticipated predictable outcomes, which produced a sense of control over my life. Constantly calculating the results reduced my risk, but it also limited opportunities for me to exercise genuine faith over unknowns. I rarely experienced real, heart-racing faith because until trouble hit my marriage, I rarely found myself in situations where I felt circumstances required it. I believed I was living a life of faith because I followed the rules, but it's probably more accurate to say I was living a life in fear of breaking them. So for me, leaving a broken marriage required even more faith than staying in one because leaving meant breaking some significant rules and expectations.

Acknowledging my fear of judgment

Our separation made me feel awkward, vulnerable, and scared. I felt out of place on my own, in a new house and a nearby town. I didn't know who I was outside of being "William's wife." Constantly cognizant that I had defied the religious rules and social expectations I had once believed in by seeking divorce, I labeled myself "divorced" in every room I walked into. Even if no one else was thinking it, there may as well have been a scarlet letter "D" pinned to my frock. *Divorced.* I struggled to understand what that meant for me. I felt shame, and I believed I needed to feel it, I deserved to feel it. At the same time, I clung to the hope that I could provide a better life for my children and myself. Wrestling with what I wanted to believe we could have versus what I perceived to be socially and religiously acceptable for a divorced woman, I took baby steps on shaky legs and wobbly knees.

In the beginning, leaving was not liberating. It was mostly terrifying. I missed the familiarity and safety of old habits, like people-pleasing for example. It required tremendous courage to challenge my nature of making sure everyone was happy with me during a time in my life when I felt very few people were. Others' expectations felt more and more like conditions I must meet in order to maintain their acceptance and approval. One such expectation was pressing in on me from a handful of people we had been closest to during our marriage, our couple-friends. Through several lengthy phone calls, a Come-to-Jesus meeting in my living room, and a few coffee dates, it was expressed to me that I should "get myself right with God and do what is best for my husband and children." I was told that I needed "to make sacrifices for my marriage," that I was "humiliating my husband" and "destroying my children's lives." I began seeing a counselor, a move that many hoped would propel me toward reconciliation with my husband. But when it didn't make the impact my closest Christian friends were hoping for, they turned their backs on me, disappointed and disapproving of the firm decision I had made to divorce.

Fear of judgment had always motivated me toward perpetual doing, propagated by guilt and anxiety. People's opinions were a measuring rod of my performance, or lack thereof, and their impending judgment incited me to do, to please, and to exceed. For years, I had hosted perfect parties, supported friends in need, and organized play dates in my home just to beat judgment to the punch. Because I was always "on," I never left any room for disapproval or dissatisfaction. But now that I was breaking rules and expectations, I was receiving a lot of reprimands and shaming from my closest friends.

Their words hurt me deeply. For the first time in my life, I managed to resist appeasing them. Still I struggled under the weight of their criticism. I carefully gathered all of their painful words and carried them around with me, as if in a backpack, so I could take them out at will and feel the punishment even I believed I deserved. My backpack was full of words that stung, thoughts that caged me in, memories of poor choices I had made, and disappointments I had caused myself and others.

It became increasingly more than I could carry. Still, I didn't set the backpack down, I just slowly took out the sticks and the stones, examined them, and gingerly laid them aside. I stopped taking calls from toxic people. I just stopped answering the phone, which was completely out of character for me because I had always made myself available to everyone. I ceased to explain myself and defend myself to people who were hurtful. One of the hardest things I did was to sit down after weeks of thought and "unfriend" scores of people on Facebook, some because they were mean and judgmental, but most because I no longer felt comfortable granting them daily access into my life because of their connection with William. Most of the latter group were part of his close circle of family and friends. They were wonderful people who did nothing wrong. However, William demonstrated no boundaries. And I needed boundaries for myself, even at the risk of disappointing people I loved, including his family. In some ways, it felt very "high school," but I couldn't ignore the lack of boundaries that existed. For the first time, I understood the privilege of privacy I was forfeiting for the sake of social media. I immediately sent a lengthy message to his family explaining how I loved them and would be happy to meet for coffee or talk some time, but I was uncomfortable with the daily contact through Facebook now that he and I were divorcing.

I know I hurt some sweet people, and I hated that. Still there were others from whom I just needed to make a clean break. They kept accosting me, and I had to end it. I did it for myself. I had to separate myself from those who would rather I measure up to their standards than support me in meeting my own. I didn't come to this decision lightly or even with disdain. I loved these people quite deeply. I believed they were genuinely doing what they thought was best. But interacting with them became incredibly painful.

Particularly as a Christian, I spent weeks pondering the shaming I was surprised to receive from so many of my close Christian friends. My experience on the receiving end of their criticism opened my eyes to how cruel Christians can be to one another. The damning phone calls, and texts, and coffees caused me to realize that I never wanted to be one of those kinds of Christians again. I was never a critical person by nature, except of myself. Still, those series of experiences made me sensitive to the ways even well-intentioned people can hack to pieces an already wounded soul.

I understood where they were coming from. After all, I once believed I was living in faith because I obeyed all the rules. I determined that their compulsion to recite the rules to me in the face of my excruciating pain ultimately came from a place of fear—their own fear of breaking the rules, of working through hard things, or maybe even of being friends with someone like me. I needed compassion, but even I didn't realize that. I believed I deserved punishment. Maybe they did too. For the most part, I was never angry with those who judged or berated me, but I did want separation from them. Their judgment, at a time when I needed their love and understanding the most, transformed my thinking about how much power I am willing to give others over the decisions I make for my life.

Letting myself receive love

Simultaneously, I was met with compassion and comfort from unexpected sources. A few women I had known for years, though not as intimately, reached out to me—not to judge, just to love on me and my kids. Most of them were mom-friends, ladies with whom I brushed shoulders at PTO meetings, school events, and the weekend birthday party circuit. They made phone calls or texts, or stopped me in the school parking lot, not to get the scoop, but to be kind and warm. A few mothers offered to pick up my children from school if I needed help since I now worked outside the home.

One such friend, Jennifer, called and sincerely said, "I hear you may be going through a hard time. What can I do for you?" Though she barely knew me, she invited me to coffee, gently inquired how I was doing, then offered to meet a need for me. She never pried into my personal life. She just listened to the little bit I was willing to share, and she offered me some personal assistant work. She treated me with dignity, not pity. It felt like sisterhood and a very warm act of Christian kindness. Her gesture was profoundly moving to me, something I will never forget.

My Carla

When my marriage ended, another person I shocked with my news of divorce was my hairdresser, Carla. I met her at a church social just months after William and I were married, and we developed a friendship in her swanky little salon. Carla was magazine-cover-stunning. She oozed with femininity and sex-appeal standing in leopard print dresses and heels all day in her flippy little salon making people look amazing. She also had a way of making people *feel* amazing from the inside out. People talked to Carla. It was more than a cliché job qualification of a hairdresser. Rather, it was a spiritual depth and warmth she exuded, dressed up in sass and confidence, that drew people to her chair like a good psychologist draws people to their sofa. She listened, she felt, and she shared. Everyone loved her, even the women who secretly wanted to hate her because she turned every head in the room.

Over the thirteen years I knew her during the course of my marriage, we connected every eight weeks when it was time to make me blonde again—or the occasional red. We had unique parallels in our lives that I could talk about with her like no one else. Over the years, we shared our intimate and uncomfortable feelings over complicated family relationships. We traded tips for being good wives and making ourselves pretty for our husbands. We connected over Sunday School classes and Bible studies we each participated in. We encouraged each other as mothers. She knew me when I was pregnant, having my babies, and setting out to be super-mom. I told her all of my proudest mommy moments. We became friends over those thirteen years, in eight-week intervals.

For my whole life, I had been so afraid of what others would think of my weaknesses and failures that I hid them. *Had I built a wall that inadvertently protected me from warm, non-judgmental people and held close the ones who judged and criticized?* My own fear of what others would think had prevented me from enjoying healthy, compassionate, fruitful relationships.

Finding faith to do it afraid

Another big fear I was facing down was determining how to immediately provide for myself and my children. I needed income. In the eight years since I had left the workforce to raise my children, I had only assisted my ex-husband in his business. When I left him, I had no income of my own, and the only professional connections I had were related to his tax and accounting business.

I felt a strong ambition toward entrepreneurship. Experienced as an executive assistant, I knew I could step back into that role, but I didn't want a regular 8-to-5 job. I preferred the autonomy of making my own hours. Most importantly, I desired to provide my children the routine they were familiar with. They were used to me taking them to school and picking them up, helping them with homework, running them to sports, and all the myriad tasks moms do with and for their children. With the upheaval divorce had shoved on them, one of my greatest priorities was to preserve as many normalcies for them as I possibly could. I wanted to work for myself.

It was likely the biggest risk I could have taken in my already vulnerable position, but with no certainty of how it would work out for me, I went for it. I decided to start my own business as an administrative and personal assistant. I began marketing to the network of small business owners I already knew. This was a huge risk for me, financially and socially. I was afraid of the potential rejection I might receive from the people I had business connections with when I began networking my own business, instead of William's. I also knew if I had a chance of launching a successful business, I would need some help paying the bills while I got it off the ground.

A "text message" from Mom

I built up the courage to share my ideas with Mom. I hated to ask for help from anyone. It seemed like an open admission that I didn't have it all together. I wanted to make my mom proud of me, not feel as if I was looking for a handout. I was so nervous when I finally asked if she would be willing to help me with rent and groceries for a few months while I tried to build my business. I explained that if in that time I couldn't create a significant client base, I would find a corporate job somewhere and move on. Mom agreed to take a chance on me—and she seemed happy about it. She believed in me, maybe in some ways like mothers naturally do, but something about her tone also made me feel she believed in me woman to woman, and entrepreneur to entrepreneur. I wasn't really expecting that. I approached her like a daughter, but she answered me like a businesswoman. She genuinely responded to my business plan, not my empty pantry (though she still snuck a peek inside my pantry and refrigerator every time she stopped by). An independent local business owner and entrepreneur herself, Mom seemed interested in my professional plans and ambitions.

She offered all kinds of encouragement along the way. Not technologically advanced, Mom left a folded piece of notebook paper under my windshield wiper blade one day. She called it a "text message." My car was parked outside of one of my new clients' office buildings. As I left work that afternoon to pick up the kids from school, I discovered the folded page flapping in the wind. The words that stuck out to me the most were, "your #1 fan." My mom was not an overly affectionate person. She rarely said things to me like "I love you," or, "I'm proud of you." I had no doubt she loved me, and I had always suspected she was "mom-proud" of me for my typical achievements like making straight As, getting married, or giving her grandchildren. But it stunned me that she could be my number one fan *now*—right in the middle of the worst failure of my life. I think she was proud of me for doing something real for myself...maybe even for being real with myself.

Launching my business

I continued networking with the same local entrepreneurs I had once marketed my ex-husband's accounting business to. I knew most of the small business owners needed administrative support but couldn't afford the expense of even a part-time employee. So I marketed myself as an independent administrative and personal assistant. Presenting my own business, to the same people I had presented my ex-husband's business to just weeks before, thrust me light years outside of my comfort zone. I could feel my heart pound and my face glow red every time I stood up in front of this community of people with whom I had developed professional relationships on his behalf. It was awkward to share just enough about my current personal situation to lend understanding about my new business endeavor without spilling out all the painful details of my home life. They were kind people, but in this professional setting, particularly as a perfectionist who liked keeping herself all buttoned-up, I felt incredibly naked and vulnerable. But week after week, I faced down my fears when we met to network. I swallowed hard, stood up again before these 20-30 people, and confidently offered my administrative services. I was thrilled to pick up new clients, and it wasn't long before I was earning an income for myself on my own terms.

In less than two months, I landed a client who was willing to give me a substantial number of hours. So, in addition to the other small clients I had acquired, I was now in a position to almost completely support myself. It meant late nights with little sleep and hustling to gain new clients while producing quality work for my existing ones. It meant being grouchy in the evenings while I made dinner and shuttled the kids through their routines. I was there to pick them up after school and there to help them with their homework, but I was constantly challenged to be present with them the way I wanted to be. It was hard to be fully engaged with them when my mind was juggling responsibilities to clients, getting the kids to basketball, scheduling appointments, and paying bills.

Some nights, after they were tucked into bed, I'd be knee deep in editing a blog or writing Facebook ads for a client, and one of my children would come stumbling out of their bedroom for a cup of water, or to just lay their head against my shoulder while I clicked away on the keyboard. Other times, I had to force myself to simply put my phone down, sit on the couch, and play a game or watch a movie with them. It was never that I didn't want to. I genuinely loved connecting with my kids. I had always savored their stories and perspectives, and I knew they needed me to help them through divorce too. It was just hard to be everything to everyone and also figure out how not to be.

Starting a business from scratch was absolutely pivotal in proving to myself that I could do a new thing without the certainty of a successful outcome. I honestly didn't know if I could pull it off, but with the support of my mother, I was able to take the risk to find out. I was gaining faith in myself and my budding independence. In the midst of doing the best I could do in the situation I was in, I found myself doing many things I had never done before. My ex-husband's words echoed in the back of my mind. When I used to try something new (or just wanted to), he liked to tell me, "You're not nearly as independent as you think you are." He would grin when he said it, like I was cute. Shame on me for wearing words that were much too small for me. They didn't fit me then, and they for damn sure don't fit me now.

Yes. Hell yes, I can do that!

I kept trying new things. I refused to let fear keep me from anything I wanted, including fear of failure. I wanted a bench swing and pretty landscaping in my backyard. So I bought myself a swing with a canopy. The gentlemen at Lowe's loaded it into my small SUV, but the box was much too heavy for me to carry from the driveway to the backyard once I got it home. So I opened the box in the back of the car, and I carried a few pieces at a time out back so I could assemble my beautiful new swing. I ran up to Home Depot to buy the tools I needed to build it. Me, with power tools—now that was empowering! It wasn't that I was too proud to ask for help. I needed to do things for myself. It felt good.

I was gaining confidence with every new thing I tried. When I envisioned something I wanted, I asked myself if I could do it. Then, I told myself, *Yes. Hell yes, I can do that!* When my garage door opener stopped working, I downloaded instructions from the internet and figured out how to fix it. I wouldn't allow myself to back down from trying something new simply because it was something I hadn't done before. I wanted to grill burgers and hot dogs and steaks for the kids and myself, but that was something William had always done. Could I do that myself? *Yes. Hell yes, I can do that!* So, I went back to The Home Depot and bought myself a pretty red grill. My seven-year-old son and I put

Andria Flores

it together on the back porch with my new power tools. When my car started making a noise, I got it repaired with the money I had saved from my new business.

"If Andria sets her mind to something, you'd best just get out of her way."

I was gaining momentum, but I hit speed bumps too. When my daughter began asking more questions about why we got divorced, I felt compelled to answer her because that's what I had always done. But something felt different now. I sensed there should probably be some boundaries and filters, but I had no idea what they were. How could I comfort her with appropriate and accurate information without putting her in the middle or adding to her stress? My son cried in bed at night because he was so torn up about Mommy and Daddy getting a divorce. He wanted a family more than anything else. My heart ached for them, wide-open and raw. I didn't know how to fix it for them. The guilt and pain snowballed, and I was emotionally wrought over how to mend our broken hearts and how to slow our tears.

Exasperated, in this too, I tried something new. I began seeking guidance from my counselor, and the kids and I gradually learned how to heal. I adopted boundaries about what I should share with my daughter and what was just for grown-up conversations. I learned how to recognize when I was being motivated by mom-guilt (or the more evil version, divorce-guilt), and still be an effective parent, one with expectations and accountability in place. Divorce was hard. Healing was even harder.

When choices had to be made in the new life the kids and I were creating, I gathered the facts and I made decisions. Though I understood that these were basic life skills people commonly engage every day, I had never done many of these things on my own before. I wasn't becoming an island unto myself, nor was I prideful or bitter. I was finding independence.

I was proving to myself that I was in fact smart enough, talented enough, and brave enough. Every time I heard Pink's song *Perfect* come on the radio, I absorbed her advice to change the voices in my head and make them like me instead. In fact, I turned it up and sang it loud through streaming tears. I added it to my Badass Playlist with the likes of Gloria Gaynor's *I Will Survive* and Natasha Beddingfield's *Unwritten*. In subtle ways, I was reprogramming my thinking from fear-based appeasing, fixing, and merely existing, to faith-filled acknowledging, decision-making, and fully living.

I found faith in myself just in doing things I had never done before. My daddy always said, "If Andria sets her mind to something, you'd best just get out of her way." As a girl, I loved it when he said that about me, but I never understood where it came from. *How did I not see this about myself?* He saw it in me when I was just a kid, and he said it to me all the way into my adulthood. So how did I miss it? I suppose I had to take a risk on myself to find out for myself. Daddy was right, I could do anything I set my mind to, but God it took a lot of courage to try.

CHAPTER 4

Approval Addiction

Always doing the right thing is a lot of work.

The more I grew as an independent woman, the more I questioned the paradigm in which I once lived. In our church circles, there had always been a lot of pressure, and subsequently great pride to be had, in having a perfect marriage. Being a good wife was deeply important to me, but it also served my need to garner the approval of others, primarily from William, but also from the people we spent our time with. Our friends respected him because he treated me so well. He showered me with flowers and diamonds I never asked for. He opened doors for me and complimented me publicly. I believe it was William's way of showing love and affection, and that it came from a sincere place, much the way my doting and doing was born of my fourth grade dream to be a good wife and mother. In a sweet way, he was proud to have me as his wife, and together we really did look as though we had a perfect marriage.

It was when the problems came that the sincere gestures we once offered became the fence we hid behind. We continued to act the part publicly in order to maintain our need for approval, but at home he resorted to his addiction, and I resorted to mine. The more time that passed after our separation and divorce, the more I seriously questioned why approval had once been so essential to me. In our marriage, I had been doing all the right things to earn his love and approval. But while I was busy making myself worthy of love, he was making himself another drink.

My performance didn't motivate him at all. It actually served to enable him. I didn't feel loved and approved for all my efforts; I felt subservient and functional. In retrospect, I can't justify my resentment with him for not seeing the real me. All I ever offered was my best performance. For thirteen years, he was married to the first-date version of me—always on, always pretty, always attentive. I had never evolved into a woman who could allow herself to be vulnerable, or real, or imperfect.

My perfectionist rock bottom

Performance had become the only way I valued myself, until it failed me of course. Then I despised the act. When I left him, we were both suddenly exposed for who we had become— actors in real life. I wish I would have seen it sooner, but in truth I genuinely believed I was doing the all the things a good wife was supposed to do. While it worked, I felt fulfilled, valued, and loved.

When it stopped working, I saw the gaping deficit of my own self-worth.

There was nothing left of the real me. I didn't even know who that was. I had lived to please other people for so long that I had morphed into an ideal, an image. My desire to be an amazing wife and mother was real, but the product was fake. Each decision I made to please someone else was like laying one more sticky, dripping strip of paper mâché onto the delicate sculpture I had formed of myself. I may have produced an appeasing image on the outside, but inside I was fragile and hollow. Once I reached the limits of what I could reasonably handle, I fractured under the weight of his problems and my pretending. The strain of William's addictions, and my inability to contain them, is what crushed me. The failure of our marriage was never entirely his fault. It was my fault too. I chose to cover. I chose to hide. I chose to placate. I was not brave enough to reach out for the help we needed, nor was I bold enough to confront our imperfections for myself.

When my flawless performance fell flat, I was angry. I sunk into despair, maybe even depression, because I couldn't do enough to save us. I felt profoundly unloved and rejected. I felt like a failure. Divorce was my unwanted, unanticipated, unwelcomed intervention into a life of pretending. It was my perfectionist rock bottom. It's where I learned I am completely imperfect, and I should embrace that about myself, not deny it or hide it.

I don't always look pretty or say the right thing. Sometimes I'm late. My kids get cranky and disheveled. I forget stuff. I'm easily distracted. I hate pant suits, but I could quite possibly live out the rest of my days in yoga pants. I laugh too loud. I don't have the answer to everything. I'm not always rainbows and butterflies. Occasionally, I get sick or just plain tired, and all I want is to lie down—and that's okay. In fact, every now and then I get good and mad, and I cuss. But for decades, my own drive to keep up appearances kept me from knowing any of this about myself, or developing who I really was as a woman...as a human.

Eventually, I realized approval is not love. Constantly striving to please and perform is not healthy for loving and respecting myself, nor does it promote healthy relationships with others. Perfectionism is not sustainable, and it is certainly not currency for love. Like any addiction, my need for approval was exhausting, and it depleted every resource in my life. Choosing to live that way, to relate to people that way, to find self-worth that way for decades had formed a tightly twisted cord around my neck, and the unraveling of it all was proving to become my lifeline out.

Sometimes doing all the right things just doesn't work.

Prior to our divorce, I was sitting in Carla's chair one day, my hair full of papers and color, when I got the courage to tell her about a less than heroic scene with my two-year-old daughter. I had taken Reese with me to check out a potential Mother's Day Out pre-school program for her. She had a complete and utter melt-down of epic proportions in front of all the ladies and children at the child care center, followed by another tantrum in the church parking lot. I was doing all the things the experts advise. I issued time outs. I whispered (while she screamed) to get her attention. I ignored her behavior and talked with the staff as if she were not screaming at the top of her lungs on the floor at our feet. I walked away, with that implied mom-dare for her to follow me. But nothing worked. I disclosed to Carla how angry and flustered I felt, and that what I really wanted to do was yank her up by the arm, swat her bottom hard, put her in the car, and take her ass home. Instead I just kept flitting around like a bird chatting with the caregivers and doing everything I thought I was supposed to do as a mother.

In response, Carla described a scene to me with her young daughter in a church restroom. Her daughter was only a year or two older than mine, and she too had thrown a tantrum at church. Many of the ladies in the restroom were looking down their noses at Carla to see what she would do to tame her seemingly unruly little girl.

Carla said, "Andria, I was frustrated. My face was hot because I knew everyone was watching to see what I would do with her. I felt the pressure to prove what a good mother I was. But, I stopped myself. I chose to do what was best for my daughter, not what would gain approving nods from the mommas and the grandmas. I didn't spank her or raise my voice. I squatted down, looked her eye-to-eye, and spoke calmly to her. Then I took her hand in mine, and we left the restroom."

It blew me away. She chose what was best for her daughter in the heat of the moment and shoved aside the burning temptation to do something more demonstrative that might gain the approval of onlookers. I know Carla; she is not afraid to spank or raise her voice. She is not mousy or ambivalent. She has made plenty of parenting mistakes and blunders, just like the rest of us. But what struck me was that she consciously made a choice for her daughter, not for the ladies in the church restroom.

Her candor compelled me to open up more about my frustrations as a mother, how hard it was to maintain my peace and control when my daughter would push all my buttons, how difficult it was to focus on her needs when I felt others looking to see what I would do next.

When I left her salon that day, having known Carla for seven years at that point, she said, "Andria, I like it that you shared your struggles. Your vulnerability is endearing. You seem real to me today. I've not seen that side of you before. It's almost like you were so perfect, I couldn't relate to you."

When I got in my car, I pulled down the visor and looked in the mirror, not to check my new hairdo, but to look myself in the eyes. All these years, I had kept myself so bound up in perfection because I believed it was part of what made people like me. I had no idea that striving to be perfect had actually made me hard to relate to. Nor did I understand how many parenting choices I had been making for others, and not actually for my children, whom I have been charged to raise.

Six years and thirty-something colors later, I sat in Carla's chair again and bravely revealed I was getting a divorce.

"Andria," she said, in the dramatic, velvety way she says my name. She put down the papers and brush full of blonde color and spun my chair around slowly to face her. "*You* are getting a divorce? *You*? I am speechless..."

A few days later, we texted to arrange a coffee date. A few weeks after that, I found myself talking to Carla on the phone on a weekly basis. A few months in, Carla had become my best friend. We made dinner plans and sat at her kitchen table or under her pergola. We talked and texted almost daily. Coffee dates with Carla could easily last three hours. Every eight weeks on average, she still made me look pretty on the outside, but our friendship...our frequent, honest, vulnerable, deep exchanges made me feel beautiful on the inside. And I was a mess!

I opened up a part of my heart that I had protected for 37 years from everyone else to the most drop-dead-gorgeous, genuine, messy, beautiful piece-of-work woman I had ever known. Carla didn't judge me. Not once. She laughed and cried with me instead. She held my hand—literally. She invited me out for girls' nights. From that point on, sitting in her chair every six to eight weeks was more like an accessory to our friendship. The genuine connection I had made with her in my heart never compared to the colors and cuts, nor did it measure against any other relationship I had ever known. I felt truly seen and loved for the whole of myself...for the parts I had never allowed to even be seen before.

"I am not worth it."

When our marriage rounded the corner toward divorce, it was because we self-destructed in our addictions. He with alcohol, and I with perfectionism. The last six months of our marriage, I cried all the time. While no one was looking, I slipped into the darkest place of my life. I cried out to him, but my cries were falling on drunk ears. My heart broken, I came to terms with the fact that my husband would not get sober for himself, for our family, or for me. In the state I was in, I internalized that to mean, *I am not worth it. We are not worth it.* I allowed those words to replay in my head because for me, they were sobering.

Dependent on his approval for so long, just like any other addict, uncurling my fingers from it was torture. During the initial period of our separation and divorce, I was still clinging to his approval with one fist and grasping at hope with the other. *We are not worth it* meant there is nothing I can do to make him choose us. For me it was detox. *I am not worth it* meant I cannot make him love me. It denied me the approval-fix I was desperate for.

Andria Flores

You are not worth it meant I had been cut off from my drug of choice. Finally, having no more open veins for approval from him, and no more resources of strength to mend our marriage, I ended it.

Releasing my drug of choice

Just like a young woman shaking on a cold hard floor, sweating out the last remnants of a drug that has held her bound, I too went through months of letting go. I had performed for love for so long, I wasn't quite sure how to be loved for who I really was. I didn't even know how to love myself without some assurance that I had earned it. I knew instinctively that this was not right, that this was not healthy, but I had a lot to learn about what was.

Moving on, I began unpacking all of the pain I had been collecting for years. I pulled it out of hiding, piece by piece. I had carried all of my negative emotions with me because I didn't know what else to do with them. I had grown up believing that expressing anger, hurt, resentment, fear, disappointment, or grief was a sign of weakness. Good girls didn't do that. So I stuffed those feelings down deep in my soul. I knew if I was going to have a chance at finding my own self-worth, I was going to need dump trucks to carry off all the crap I had been piling on. Getting to a place of wholeness and authenticity would mean unloading all of the pain I had carefully concealed. So I took on the daunting task of clearing out the negative emotions and hurtful situations I hadn't dealt with in my life.

Sometime after I moved into our rental house, I connected with an old friend I had grown up with since the second grade. As children, we had lived five houses down from one another. Here we were 30 years later, discovering that we literally lived five minutes from each other in a different town from where we had been raised. In terms of personality, Danielle was my opposite. She was the extrovert; I was the introvert. She was the center of all the attention I shunned. She was bright and funny and silly. I was studious and serious and controlled.

So much life had been lived since high school, and here we were now walking and running around the track together at the community center a few evenings a week. We'd meet up with our tenny-shoes on and walk and talk as the sun went down. She too was going through a divorce, and we listened to each other with the familiar love and acceptance of childhood. Some days, she'd come over, and we'd curl up in blankets on my sofas and drink coffee and sort out the meaning of life and love, or just laugh like the little girls we once were. We hauled off dump truck loads of shame, hurt, and fear.

While I was slowly building courage to share hard things with my closest friends, Carla and Danielle, my journal became my constant companion. It was a safe place to express exactly what I was thinking and feeling, to find the words to describe how

I truly felt, rather than the scripted ones I had once written or spoken aloud. The pages became a quiet retreat where I could pray and think. I challenged myself to be raw in a way I was not really comfortable with, but that I needed. In the past, when I had journaled, or even prayed, I always presented the best version of myself. Even in those sacred places, I didn't feel safe enough to be authentic.

I didn't want to live that way anymore. So, I got real. I cussed. I told myself, and I told God, how pissed off I was. I acknowledged just how deeply I hurt, even though the admission felt like weakness. My marriage was over, so I grieved the loss of the lifestyle I had with my husband and children. Getting all of that out of my heart and onto paper made me keenly aware of how vulnerable and scared I felt about the future.

But I just kept writing. I kept talking to God. I kept connecting with my closest friends. One dump truck after another, I gradually off-loaded years of pain and resentment, piles of disappointment and heartaches, and heaps of unrealistic expectations —and that's when I found it. Clearing out layer upon layer of negative thinking and unhealthy doing, I discovered my self-worth beginning to glow through the rubble.

I had been a junkie for approval.

Approval had meant love to me. But, no more. Whether it had been cheap paper awards on my parents' kitchen wall; raises, promotions, or special recognition from employers; or fulfilling others' expectations and supporting others' dreams, I unwittingly put myself in personal and professional relationships over and over again in which I could earn more approval, or ultimately a counterfeit of love. It's hard to believe that I really thought I had to earn love. In my mind, I knew this was not how love works. But in reality, it's how I lived. It's how I performed in relationships.

Following our divorce, and in the absence of my ex-husband's approval, I was thrust into a brand-new place of thinking for myself and doing things for myself. I had no idea the impact simply trying new things for myself would have on my innate drive to please others. While it was freeing, the transition into doing things on my own was also uncomfortable and taxing. Filtering daily choices through the eyes of others was familiar and easy for me. My new practice of making decisions by myself and for myself demanded tremendous emotional and mental energy. I an over-thinker to begin with, but being single really challenged me to push aside my addiction for approval (especially from my ex-husband), and think through hard questions I hadn't confronted before. *Can I do that? Can I have that?* And perhaps the most exacting question, *What do I want?*

A handful of first dates

Throughout our separation and divorce, I don't know that I ever saw myself re-marrying. It's not that I ruled it out; I just hadn't thought that far ahead yet. I fixated on what I needed to do

Andria Flores

in the moment to help my children, to develop my career, and to just feel whole as a woman. That didn't leave much time to over-think a romantic life, and it certainly didn't leave much opportunity for actual dates. I think that's how I sort of stumbled into a handful of first dates. Rather first, there was a lot of texting—because apparently texting is the new dating. There was a lifeguard, an attorney, an IT guy, even a couple of retired men who thought they were on dates with me, all the while I legitimately believed we were networking our businesses over coffee. It got comical.

I had exchanged business cards with the IT guy because I needed help with a blog I had started. It was called *Lonely Girl Patio Tour*. It's what I did when I went out on solo dates to patio restaurants. I watched people, I wrote, and I fumbled around online trying to figure out how to start a blog. Initially, I felt as if I were fulfilling a personal dare to myself, sitting at restaurants enjoying a drink or a meal alone. But over time it became a very enriching habit and healing for my soul. I learned firsthand, *not everyone is looking at me. I am not under a microscope. I can do something I enjoy for myself without giving thought to what anyone might think about me. In fact, they're not. They're not thinking about me, or judging me, or even wondering what I'm doing at a restaurant alone.* It was good for me.

The IT guy was much younger than I, and it was clear after one conversation that I needed technical support. So when he called a few days later to offer his expertise, I had no reason to believe it was anything but professional. He was using words like URL, domain, and WordPress, and I was trying to keep up. So when he blurted out, "You have the most beautiful eyes I've ever seen," I literally laughed out loud. *Was he flirting with me?* Why, yes. Yes, he was…which led to two weeks of texting. I remember thinking, *how long do we text before we actually go out?* So I finally asked him myself if he'd like to meet up for coffee.

Coffee seemed like a small commitment. Coffee is brief. After all, how long can a coffee date last, right? The IT guy turned out to be the Longest. Coffee. Date. Ever. He was a very kind-hearted guy, but somewhere toward the bottom of my skinny vanilla latte, he started telling me about dubstop. Wait, is it *dubstop*? Or *dubstep*? I had to use the context clues just to know it was a form of music. It sounded to me like the little rubber wedge used to hold a door open. When he excused himself to the restroom, I Googled it to figure out what the hell he was talking about, and I still didn't know.

We ended up sitting in my car outside of the Starbucks so he could play some of it for me. It sounded like noise—seriously, just noise. It was an hour and a half into the date (so like 9 PM). I was tired, I didn't get his music, and I wanted to leave, but he was still in my car. I felt…old. So I drove him over to his car, but he still didn't get out. I finally had to tell him honestly, "Thank you for meeting me for coffee. I am tired now and ready to go home."

It was a lengthy coffee date, but a quick lesson on first dates, younger men, and dubstep. It's *dubstep.*

Perhaps the most valuable lesson I learned was that I had choices. I could choose whether or not I date. I could choose with whom I spent my time. I could choose to say *yes,* or I could choose to say *no, thank you*—even to a cute 20-something IT guy, a hot lifeguard from the pool, or a charming young attorney. Not every relationship was deep, or long, or serious, but each one was meaningful.

My handful of first dates all taught me something. It wasn't un-lady-like to ask him out first. It wasn't mean to move on. I didn't need to try to make a boy like me. If I saw something I wanted, I could go for it. I could be kind and warm *and* up front. I didn't know I had those freedoms before. I was raised as a Southern Christian girl who believed I always had to put the other person first, nod in agreement, and submit without regard to how I felt about all that. I went from being one man's daughter to another man's wife. I learned to please and submit.

Ultimately, it was how I gained approval. Even I couldn't believe I had spent so much of my life working so hard for love— from men, from parents, from friends, even from God. I must have been good at it though, because I rarely felt unloved. I was happy for most of my life, and I had never given conscious thought to what I was doing to create that for myself. But I was beginning to see that I believed I must prove myself worthy of love.

CHAPTER 5

Busy Is Not a Badge of Honor

A moment of clarity

A few months after I separated from William, I made this raw entry in my journal. It became for me a moment of clarity, a lighthouse to look to when I lost my way or felt sucked into routines, and tasks, and function. To this day, it still reminds me of who I am and who I want to be.

> *...embracing the gentle soulfulness, the creativity, the quiet, reflective spirit in me that I buried along the way...shamefully hiding what was important to me—what I valued of my own soul—to make room for and develop what was important to everyone else: function. I am so much more than that. I am more than a scheduler, a cheerleader, a lunch-maker, a sexual-pleaser, a planner, a peace-maker, a soother, an organizer, a problem-solver, a prayer warrior, a people-pleaser.*

There is more depth to me than keeping everyone else's lives running smoothly, without inconvenience or burden. I am a beautiful, quiet soul. I think deeply. I feel deeply. I want. I need. I laugh. I love. I dream. I express. I hurt. I cry. I don't just give; I take. I'm not just functional; I am passionate! I am spiritual, not religious. I am not afraid of who I am or what I want, nor am I ashamed. I like me.

I had built a marriage—in fact, I had built most every relationship in my life—on what I had to offer. Extremely uncomfortable with anything that felt like taking, I conditioned myself to constantly give. It's no secret that eventually I needed to refill my own tank, but I didn't know how. My idea of refueling meant ardently studying scripture and devoting hours to prayer. Though feeding my spirit could certainly be a means of reprieve and peace, I used them as tools to work out answers to my problems, or more often someone else's. My faith was just another thing I worked at. I prayed incessantly for my husband and children. I prayed for friends or acquaintances at church. I prayed for victims of traffic accidents as we passed them on the freeway. Even my prayer-life was driven by doing.

As a young mother, I remember being consciously aware that my physical body rarely felt like my own anymore. It was literally functioning for the other three people in my house. At one point, between nursing my infant son, carting around my two-year-old daughter on my hip, making myself available sexually to my husband, and pack-muling diaper bags, car seats, and strollers, I was physically depleted. All three of them grabbed and groped at me night and day, and I felt guilty for even feeling that way. I secretly relished any rare moment I could sneak off and take a nap or a shower and not be touched. I am by nature a physically affectionate person, but I was over-stimulated and under-rested. I loved my family dearly, but with everything I carried, I eventually began to feel unappreciated and unnoticed. When I made that entry in my journal years later, it was the culmination of 13 years of marriage and eight years of motherhood—all dedicated to seeing the people I loved most succeed. I devoted myself to them entirely. It's no wonder I grew tired and resentful.

How did my lifelong dream of being a wife and a mother turn into knots in my shoulder and fantasies of going to the bathroom by myself? When did the shift occur from a selfless, sincere desire to love and serve my family to a frustrated, exhausted young woman? I felt as if I was doing all the right things a wife and mother were meant to do, but I didn't like how I was being treated. I wanted to be noticed and appreciated for what I contributed. I was always buzzing around the house, so why did I feel so invisible to them? I reasoned I must need to try harder, so I took on more. I set out to prove my value by what I could do for them, but no amount of sacrifice or tasks seemed to be enough. I felt less and less like a woman, and more and more like a well-oiled machine. *Why couldn't they see me?*

Oprah Winfrey once said, "You train people how to treat you." I was responsible for how I allowed myself to be treated. Relationships require at least two people. We each brought something to the table, and we each consumed something while we were there. I cannot hold other people entirely responsible if I feel mistreated, taken for granted, used, or unseen. Ultimately, it was on me to decide how I should be treated. My husband, my children, even my closest friends at the time treated me the way I conditioned them to. It took years for me to see that, but eventually I realized I didn't like the way I had taught the people in my life to interact with me. I didn't know how to change that immediately, but I knew instinctively I needed to figure it out.

I wore Busy like a badge of honor.

Walking through the threshold of divorce transformed me from a busy wife and mother to an even busier single-mom. I gave myself to my children without boundaries because I was drowning in divorce-guilt. Neither had I learned to enforce boundaries with my ex-husband. I had absolutely zero margins in my life. I worked late into the night and started early the next morning, and I worked while the kids were at school. I learned to manage a home, a job, and children completely on my own, which are common responsibilities every single parent is taxed with. I had traded the stress of a failing marriage for the stress of a single parent. I absolutely did not want to be pitied, but I won't pretend—it was just plain hard. However, like many single parents will also attest, I was highly motivated because I wanted to build a new life for my children and myself. I knew we could make it, so for the first time in my life, I slid into the driver's seat. Gradually, tentatively, I stopped waiting to see what my ex-husband would say or do, and I took care of our children and myself first.

As exhausted as I was, I persevered on the fuel of inspiration and the fumes of desperation. Whenever my parents would call, or friends would reach out and ask how I was doing, I accurately responded, "Busy." It was like proof in one word that I got this. My ironclad work ethic served us well. I would get up at 5:00 AM and work, then get the kids up at 6:30 AM to get ready for school. After I dropped them to school, I could work again from 9:00 AM until 3:00 PM, when it was time to go pick them up. Once we were finished with sports, homework, dinner, and baths, I would tuck them in and start working again at 9:00 PM. On a good night, I'd be in bed by midnight. On the days the kids were with their dad, I would work 12-15 hour days just to get it all in. I would go months this way without taking a single weekday or weekend off. Occasionally, I might take a few hours to have dinner at a patio restaurant, go out with friends, or even less seldom have a date on a Friday or Saturday night. Usually, I just worked. One of my new friends called working on Friday night, "pulling an Andria."

After my handful of first dates, I met someone who was worth a second. Carla introduced me to Os. (His name rhymes with *pause*.) He made it past the coffee date. In fact, we just kept going on mores dates. Os was my age, though he liked to remind me I am almost exactly one year older than him. He had the good looks and texting skills of those younger guys, but didn't lack the courage to ask me out. He had the maturity and wisdom of those older men, but unlike them, he made his intentions clear. Os was a gentleman whether anyone was looking or not. He picked me up for our first dinner date, and he even helped me change a light bulb that was broken and jammed in the socket. He thought I was badass for mowing my own yard and owning my own business. He told me how attractive I was for being both independent and tender-hearted. He thought I was smart and funny. In fact, the number of times he told me those things far outweighed the number of times he told me I was pretty—and I liked that. When I was out with Os, he didn't treat me like a princess; he treated me like a lady, like an equal—and I loved that.

So when Os asked for more dates, I said *yes*. The thing is, he was in the same season of life as me. His divorce began only months before mine. He was rebuilding his own life with two young children, nearly the same ages as mine. And he too, had an astonishing work ethic, all of which meant not a lot of time for dates. But that was perfect, as neither of us was in a hurry to go anywhere fast in our personal lives. Os worked in law enforcement

Andria Flores

in the same city my father had retired from as a firefighter. We later discovered Os had begun his career with the city the same month and year Daddy had retired. I enjoyed getting to know him. We both shared the same concern about getting into a serious relationship too soon, but I sure did like him.

My primary focus though was to get the kids and me somewhere better than where we were at the time. I was willing to do whatever it took to make a better life for us, so I took pride in my ambition and ability to get things done. I was discovering daily how much I loved doing things for myself, especially working for myself. By this time, I had uncovered a dormant passion for writing. One of my new clients with a leadership organization, contracted me to work full-time for him. Wes was a local physician who was passionate about personal growth and organizational leadership. We worked well together on his writing projects and leadership blog. Because he was so committed to seeing the people in his circles succeed, he was a Godsend in my life. I wanted to succeed, and Wes consistently encouraged me to try new things professionally. He even routinely set me up to meet incredible mentors and coaches. I cherished the autonomy this position afforded me as well as the opportunity to hone my writing and editing skills. I worked very hard to grow myself and my business, and I was proud of how diligently I worked and saved and built. At some point though, I had to face the fact that while this 60-hours-a-week pace for my handful of clients may be admirable at best, it was absolutely not sustainable. My body told me so.

One year after the separation from my ex-husband, the stress and my pace were catching up with me. I was struggling with debilitating pain in my neck and shoulders. I was exhausted, and I knew that five hours of sleep a night was not enough, but I felt incapable of changing my schedule. I also knew working from a laptop all day and night was straining my body, but it was the nature of my occupation. So I drank more coffee and alternated Advil and Tylenol so I could power through. *Busy* had become a badge of honor. *Busy* meant I was earning respect and money, and hustling to make a life for us. Besides caffeine, I thrived on inspirational quotes and words like: *hustle, power through,* and *make it happen.* But there is no balance in *busy,* and my body finally had enough.

One afternoon on the couch with my laptop, I stopped. Something was wrong, and it scared me. Besides the chronic pain in my neck and shoulders, I was getting sharp pains in my stomach. I felt light-headed and dizzy. I drove myself to the doctor. When I arrived, I was on the verge of passing out and literally required help walking down the hall to the exam room, which completely embarrassed me. Tests revealed I had a kidney infection and bleeding ulcers in my stomach. I had not been not taking care of myself. I had overmedicated my neck/shoulder pain, and I was not getting adequate sleep. Basically, I redlined my body by keeping the throttle floored. Somewhere along the way, I had crossed a line from "doing what I had to do in the situation I was in" to outright martyrdom. I was not healthy, and I was frustrated that the doctor was instructing me to take time to rest and heal. I didn't have time for that. Besides, resting had always felt like laziness to me, which I despised.

Os brought me soup and a movie that Friday night after he got off work and got his children settled with a babysitter. My children were with William. I asked Os to stay for a little while, to sit with me on the couch and watch the movie with me. I couldn't believe he was willing to go to all that trouble to pick up his children and get them settled, pay for a sitter, and get dinner and a movie just to come across town to check on me and care for me—and he wasn't even going to stay. He wanted to let me rest. *Who does that?* He called his sitter and made arrangements to stay long enough to watch the movie with me. I was sick, and I was exhausted. I wasn't pretty, and I wasn't sun-shiny. Yet, this man was so loving and respectful to me. I felt seen and genuinely cared for.

I stopped drinking coffee and wine for eight weeks. I eliminated all pain medications. I ate bland foods and drank extra water. I prayed to God, and I cussed the kidney infection. Apparently, the latter technique does not promote healing. It took over two months to get over the damned thing. I consented to let my kids stay extra days here and there with their dad or with my mother so I could lie down and get the rest I needed. And of course, I worked. My doctor told me later that had I carried health insurance, he would have admitted me to the hospital for a few days of intensive antibiotic treatment. Instead, I rested at home, worked, took naps…and shored up the final terms of my divorce.

The legal aspect of divorce—that was the most stressful thing on my shoulders. It was over a year before our divorce was finalized. My attorney offered little guidance in writing the terms, so I composed most of it myself. My soon-to-be-ex-husband fought me every step of the way, so there was little to no negotiating with him. He was determined that we should remain married, that I would always be his wife, no matter what the State of Texas said. He would agree to meet with me under the guise of ironing out the terms of our divorce. But because I grossly lacked boundaries, I let myself get sucked into his unrelenting religious manipulation, guilt-ridden phone calls, and useless meetings to talk about the kids. I didn't shield myself from his venomous words because a part of me still believed I deserved them for leaving in the first place. So I'd let him pile them on. I would sit there and take it and cry incessantly because I thought it was my cross to bear. Then I would run home and ask God to tell me again who I really was.

Addictions aren't easy to break. Because I had been addicted to William's approval over anyone else's, receiving his religious reprimands and scolding speeches was like putting a needle to my vein and ripping it away every time. I didn't want that drug, but in a shameful way I still needed it. On top of the demands of my work, and the divorce papers, and being a single-parent, I hadn't learned to create the boundaries I needed and deserved, so I continued to react to every fire by jumping in with both feet to put them out. Only, I just ended up consumed in the flames myself. My body may have forced me to stop and rest, but my lingering health issues made it clear that I didn't know how to adequately manage the stress in my life.

"I am free."

The dewy spring morning our divorce was finally signed off on in court, I felt relieved. When it was all over, I stood on my back porch with the sun radiating on my face, closed my eyes over warm tears, and inhaled. I dropped my shoulders and softly exhaled, "I am free." I finally felt free to put submission and function behind me. "I am free." I just kept whispering *I am free* until a small smile emerged through my tears.

Eliminating the weekly business of negotiating our divorce reduced my stress level considerably. However, I knew I would continue to be exhausted if I didn't manage other stressors and get more sleep. I wanted to improve my quality of life. Since I didn't readily see a viable way to adjust my schedule for work and for my children, I determined to make a shift in my thinking from time-management to value-management. Rather than reacting to demands on my time by putting out fires, I set out to determine what I valued most and make everything else work around that. I wanted to free up more time for resting and thinking, and more time for my growing passion to write. I wanted to be fully present with my kids when I had them, not just make it through the nightly cycle of soccer, homework, dinner, baths, and bedtimes.

The school year ended before I knew it, and I spent the summer of 2013 looking for ways to simplify the way the kids and I spent our time and money. I spent more time outdoors. I ran through the sprinkler with them on the side of the house. I scheduled more face-to-face time with my friends. I drove the kids and me to East Texas to visit my dad and stepmom for a long weekend. I chose to look for and appreciate small things. I prayed more open-endedly, like conversations with God where I gave equal time to listening. I cultivated gratitude for the people in my life and the moments I had been taking for granted. Once I identified what mattered most to me, what I truly valued, I made quality decisions to put those things first. Only then did I begin to effectively manage my time and start to minimize stress. I found fulfillment when I acknowledged what I valued, then arranged my time to support my values.

Value management

It took the entire summer for me to retrain my thinking. But as August waned, I was sleeping seven hours a night, sometimes more. I cuddled the kids up with me on the sofa. We made popcorn and cookies together. I laughed and danced with them in the kitchen. We took walks, grilled hot dogs, and played outside. We laid on the backyard swing together, read books, and took selfies. We shared secrets and made pinkie-promises that we'd always be this close.

Once school was in full swing, I was able to creatively arrange my work schedule around us, rather than arranging us around work. I still worked several nights a week and over the weekends when the kids were with their dad. I had to in order to work full-time hours and still pick the kids up from school each day. But now I limited the time I worked, and when I didn't work, I forced myself to focus on the kids and the present moment, rather than obsess over what I still needed to get done. It wasn't always ideal, nor did I get it right every time, but it was a huge step forward after sustaining an unhealthy schedule for eighteen months straight.

I also made time for a few more dates—with Os, of course. Between the two of us, with our careers, and children, and new schedules with our exes, we had to be creative and intentional if we wanted to spend time with one another. Most weekends my kids were with their dad. I wrote the visitation terms in such a way that I could keep their weekday school routines as consistent as possible because I wasn't sure yet that he would. He was still battling his own addiction, the best I could tell. Os, on the other hand, had his children almost every weekend because he and his ex-wife devised a schedule to accommodate their careers.

One weekend Os asked me out to dinner, and then for coffee. I knew he had to hire a sitter in order to make that happen. A babysitter for two children is expensive, so I took the opportunity to take the check at dinner when the waitress came by. I immediately felt self-conscious about what I had done. I only wanted to be kind, to help offset the cost of our date that evening. But I suddenly realized I may have offended him by making that move. Afterall, he was the man, and I wasn't sure how he would feel about a woman buying him dinner.

I looked at him cautiously and asked, "Is that okay? I know you're having to pay for a sitter tonight, and I would love to buy us dinner."

He graciously responded, "You don't have to do that." But the smile on his face revealed his gratitude and respect, and he let me have the check.

I liked that, and I could tell he did too. I wouldn't have received that response in my marriage with William. He would have found it offensive for the woman to pay. I think I surprised Os. I think I surprised myself a little bit, too. I was falling in love with Os. I was attracted to his warmth, his intellect, and his integrity. I knew early on that if things didn't work out for us romantically at some point, Os was the kind of person I would want to be friends with forever. He's just one of those people who adds value to others, and I loved watching him do that.

White space

By the end of December, when the kids were out for Christmas Break, in the middle of gathering for family Christmases and holiday activities, I was living a schedule—that while still very full—now supported my values. What's more, I was learning the value of margins, literally time that was not appointed for tasks or productivity, not even for my children or my friends. I was learning to create space for rest and for no plans at all.

In order to create margins in my life, I literally made empty space on my calendar. Margins helped me effectively honor the time expressly blocked for rest and relaxation. It was like an appointment I made with myself. Because I honored that time as if it were an appointment, creating margins reduced the busy clutter and noise of overcommitment. My need to impress others by saying *yes* continued to diminish as I found more value in myself and reduced my need for approval from others. If time was blocked on my calendar for working out, reading, or watching a movie, I rarely had trouble turning down an opportunity to volunteer at the school or take on additional projects. What I valued most was already scheduled on my calendar—even the margins. I'm not saying there were never exceptions, but I learned to respect the margins.

I recall in elementary school, we were scolded if we wrote in the margins of our notebook paper, the empty white space on either side of the red vertical lines. The margins were to be kept clear of our work. Once I learned to type, I set one-inch margins in Word as a standard default. Occasionally, I could adjust them by a point or two just to squeeze everything into one page. I could pull that off in life every now and then, too. But if I allowed myself to do that all the time, I would fall back into my old, unhealthy habit of forcing everything to fit. It would prove to be too much for the space it had been given. I finally understood that I must respect the white space, the unscheduled moments of my days and weeks. I needed to give myself an inch to breathe, to rest, to reflect, and to live. Once I understood that, when family or friends asked how I was doing, I would cringe if the word *busy* left my lips. It was no longer a badge of honor to me. It was a giant neon sign that somewhere my values were not aligned. It was a nudge on my heart that my value as a person was not contingent on how well I performed, but on my character and principles.

CHAPTER 6

You Think You're So Perfect

"You think you're so perfect."

Actually, that's the problem. I don't. Being called a *teacher's pet, goody-two-shoes, excellent role model,* or *perfect example* never made me feel proud. It made me feel shame. The very goals and images I chased in my pursuit of perfection often left me in tears once I achieved them. My motivation was misplaced. I didn't pursue goals for myself, but rather for the approval of others. Whether I succeeded or failed, I nearly always felt some level of shame or rejection. Naturally, failure was humiliating because of the exposure. But quite honestly, success was humiliating for the same reason. I didn't want the limelight, and I hated being judged as perfect.

One particular semester of third grade, I was quietly beaming all the way home from school because I knew what was inside my backpack: a straight-A report card. Once my siblings and I let ourselves into our house, we began comparing report cards as we scavenged the kitchen for afterschool snacks. When it was my turn to share, my joy was quickly squashed by their teasing and ridicule.

"You think you're so perfect."

"You're such a teacher's pet!"

"Goody-two-shoes! You're going to ruin it for the rest of us when Mom and Dad get home."

They were kids too, doing what kids do, but it didn't slow the sharp sting of humiliation rising all the way up from my belly, through my chest, and onto my heated face, producing tears of shame. I wanted to hide—everything—my face, my grades, my tears.

In my bedroom, I sobbed and prayed to be invisible. I had to get my report card signed and returned to school the next day, so I couldn't just hide it from my parents. I didn't know what to do. I honestly don't remember how it went that evening when they signed everyone's report cards, with one exception. I was singularly focused on downplaying my straight As like it was no big deal. *Just get in, and get out.* I didn't want a pat on the back or a "We're so proud!" I just wanted to go unnoticed.

The next morning, when we were dropped off early at Harrison Lane Elementary, I made a beeline for my locker, face down. I wanted to get rid of that report card as quickly as possible, to turn it in to Mrs. Sebastian and never ever have to see it again. I hadn't let my parents see me cry because I didn't want them to ask me what was wrong and force me to shed any light whatsoever on the exchange with my siblings. I refused to draw any further attention to them (or to my grades) because I didn't want them to be angry or tease me anymore. So, the moment I stepped foot into the school hallway, I burst into the myriad tears I had been holding back all morning. It was the third-grade ugly cry: wet face, puffy eyes, and stringy snot. I hated the reaction that success had brought. I never wanted to feel like that again. Never. Ever. Ever.

Mrs. Stroud, a fourth grade teacher, stopped me in the hall. I didn't know her yet, but I had heard she was really mean. With her hand firmly gripping my shoulder, she steered me into an empty classroom, lights still off, and made me tell her why I was crying. She wasn't the type to pat you on the back and send you on your way. My weak little, "I'm okay," wasn't going to cut it with her. She wanted to know the truth. *The truth?* A fragile façade of perfection is no match for the ugly truth—or for Mrs. Stroud. So, I spilled it.

I was bracing for her to bark at me to "dry it up" and send me on to class. But I think she would have liked to swat them all with her big paddle. She knew our whole family, so I wouldn't have put it past her. Instead, she consoled me. She told me I needed to do my personal best without regard to what anyone else thinks. She encouraged me to be proud of myself because I put in the work. She said all the right things to me that morning in that dark, vacant classroom—things I needed to hear. God in Heaven,

I wanted to let myself believe her! But the shame I felt was so huge, so pressing, I just couldn't let go of my fear and believe.

I never thought I was perfect. I struggled my entire life because I was keenly aware that I wasn't. I strived to achieve unattainable goals and exceed impossible standards to prove to myself that I was. Then I worked dutifully to perfect my outward image when I inevitably fell short. Like an underweight girl who forces herself not to eat because she sees herself as fat and ugly, I forced myself to appear perfect because I knew better than anyone that I was not. It's torture. The thing I was driven most in life to attain was also my albatross.

Losing control at Chicken Express

Throughout my life I didn't want to just *look* as though I had myself all together, I wanted to *actually* have it all together. I invested considerable energy into making myself look good, my children look good, my home and my marriage look good. When something didn't go the way I envisioned, I'd unravel and become frustrated. I usually tried to stuff those emotions down deep and pretend everything was just fine.

I remember one Mother's Day when William and I were still married and our children were small. I had planned to pick up fried chicken after church and head to the city's botanic gardens, as had become our Mother's Day tradition. We would enjoy a leisurely picnic, walk around and take in the scenery, play with the children, feed the fish in the koi pond, and capture beautiful photos. I had built up a dreamy vision for myself of how the day would unfold.

I should have given up the dream at the fast-food chicken joint. My two-year-old son wouldn't sit still while we waited for our to-go order, and he was pitching a fit every time I insisted that he did. My arms were locked around his squirming, kicking body, my dress getting crumpled, and my hair disheveled. My four-year-old daughter whined, "I don't want fried chicken! I want McDonald's!" She drew further attention to our crumbling scene while we waited impatiently for our chicken. I could feel the heat rising in my body. I was embarrassed that my children were acting out. They were ruining *my* Mother's Day!

I was keenly aware of all the judging eyes peering at me. Those people had to be thinking what a terrible mother I was. Though the restaurant barely had anyone in it, I felt as if a hundred people were staring at us. The energetic kids, their kicking, and their whining was more than I could control. I had enough, so I started telling them through clinched teeth, "It's *Mother's* Day! Be good for Mommy. *Mommy* wants fried chicken and a picnic because it's *MOTHER'S DAY!*" The kids were two and four. Two and four. They were acting like hungry, wiggly two and four year olds. William stared blankly at me. He said, "You always build up fantasies about how something is going to be, and then you get frustrated when it doesn't turn out the way you imagined." He was exactly right, but I didn't see it that way at all. I saw *my Mother's Day* being *ruined.*

As a perfectionist, I made choices from a position of self-preservation, not literal survival of course, but keeping up appearances, preserving an image I could live with. In that regard, I suppose I thought a lot about myself, about the image I wanted to achieve. So I worked feverishly to maintain and tweak my own ideal of perfection. When I thought about others, most of the time it was in my relentless pursuit of approval. I was driven by my constant concern of what others thought about me. The more imperfect I felt, the harder I worked to attain perfection. I didn't know how to be normal without perfection or how to be loved without approval. Riddled with anxiety when I made mistakes, failed, or simply felt out of control at Chicken Express, I fought fiercely to cover, pretend, and regain control of my image.

Once on my own however, with the divorce behind me, my children beginning to adapt to our new normal, and a budding new relationship for me, life was showing me that I had not cornered the market on control. Bad things happen, sometimes devastating things outside of my control. That does not make me a bad person, nor does it mean my faith is lacking. It's just the way life rolls. The smaller my shame from divorce appeared in my rearview mirror, the more freedom I felt to relax my grip on controlling the future. I was learning to stop holding my breath and gripping the wheel.

One of the things Os shared with me regarding how he saw our relationship was that there was no finish line. I don't know that I had ever been comfortable without an end-goal and all the steps laid out to get there. So while having no finish line felt uncomfortably open-ended, it was also a gift to me. It was a gift to relinquish the responsibility to plan and measure. It was a gift to remove the pressure to perform. I never felt that way with him anyway. While many aspects of my life, like my children and my writing career, required much dedication, planning, and action, my relationship with Os was a place I could breathe. He had a soothing effect on me, which is ironic because our type A overachiever personalities are quite similar. With Os though, I felt safe to relax. We shared equal responsibility for the future of our relationship without the pressure to plan it all out.

I was an OCD Martha.

Keeping it together is a tireless cycle. By nature, perfectionism means constantly fixing or hiding imperfection. This makes me somewhat of a clean-freak. The first time Os was in my home, he asked, "Is your place always this clean and neat?" I laughed. I despise clutter and mess. My family knows if they set their glass down too long, I'm likely to pick it up and put it in the dishwasher. If something in the house is not currently in use—right this minute—I'm either going to put it away or throw it away. *Clearly, I am a joy to live with.*

The truth is, I do this for me. It's an insatiable urge to stay busy and keep clean. Especially when I am under stress, the tangible acts of folding clothes, dusting furniture, and washing dishes is my OCD way of controlling my environment when I know I can't control my circumstances. It's my way of making some things perfect when other things are not. So I do this dance of cleaning and straightening to satisfy my own need for control.

It's hard to sit still, sometimes even to engage with the people I love, so I keep moving. I sincerely don't want to make people uncomfortable with my constant tidying, but unless I make a conscious effort not to, I do. I get caught being a Martha much more often than a Mary. The Bible story of these two sisters always challenged me. It's a little intimidating how an OCD woman named Martha opened her immaculate home to *the* perfect man, Jesus Christ. It makes me a little dumbstruck to imagine both her excitement and crazy-anxiety. Martha was in overdrive preparing a fancy lunch, which she undoubtedly served on her nicest dishes for Jesus and His people. She then cleared the table and made room for coffee and dessert. She was buzzing about, everything under control, with her fixed smile and polite laughter. But inside she was boiling because her sister, Mary, was just sitting there at the feet of Jesus, hanging on His every word. *Must be nice.* But Martha continued to prove her importance through service, perfect service.

Andria Flores

Finally, she had enough, and she told Jesus, "Don't you care that I'm doing all the work while Mary just sits there? Tell her to help me!"

Jesus calmly responded, "Martha. OCD Martha. Your mind is racing with a thousand things—all competing for importance. But Mary has gotten still. She has chosen what's best."

Every perfectionist and overachiever's worst nightmare…she didn't just miss the mark of perfection, someone else did it better than her, and none other than Jesus Christ Himself called her out on it. Martha missed the point.

Sometimes I am Martha. Well, more times than I'd like to admit. I genuinely love people, family gatherings, and laughter with friends. I mean, my heart is so full of love for people it often gives me tears, and I'm too much with the hugs. But if I don't make a conscious effort to sit my ass down and engage, I totally miss the point. I have to be intentional, or I will default to perfection over presence every single time, and I don't like that about myself. It doesn't authentically reveal who I desire to be; it reveals who I default to be.

Keeping it between the lines

My drive to obey the rules, to meet or exceed expectations, is innate. I have always thrived once I understood the rules and boundaries. When I was 16 and first learning to drive, my dad took me out on the freeway for the first time in our big family Suburban. I didn't have my bearings yet of how it felt to keep that big vehicle between the lines. I remember coming up the entrance ramp on Highway 121 and asking him, "How do I know if I am keeping it in my lane?" Daddy responded, "A good indicator is to keep the Chevy hood ornament in line with the stripes on the road." So I followed his directions to the letter. Dad swallowed hard after we got home and I proudly revealed I had stared at that hood ornament the entire time we were on the freeway.

My comfort zone is between the lines. Given a rule, a guideline, or an expectation, I will make it my mission to meet or exceed it. Until now, on the backside of divorce, I never would have dreamed of off-roading, of drifting outside the lines of social expectations and religious rules. I lived my life between the lines as a child, a teenager, a wife, a mother, and a Christian woman because that's what I thought people expected of me, and it's what I expected of myself. It made my life acceptable, predictable, and comfortable. Breaking the rules was a total departure from my style. So, divorce seemed like a hard right turn off the freeway.

During the last year or so of my marriage, as I awakened to the fact that I was living a lie, I noticed that people looked at us like, "You're so perfect." I recalled that during the pregnancy of our first child, one of our very closest friends told us, "You guys are living the American Dream. You're like the perfect all-American family: happily married, working in ministry, living in a beautiful home, having your first baby..." I felt like a million bucks! I thought, *Wow! He's right. This is everything I ever dreamed of!* Then, one year later on our anniversary trip to Mexico, William started drinking, and he didn't stop.

Seven years after that, he still hadn't stopped. That's when something finally broke in me. When my marriage ended, I felt like a fraud. We had faked it for a very long time. But "fake it til you make it" is the makings of bullshit. If you aren't making mistakes, you are faking it. When I left William, I didn't think I was perfect. I loathed who I had become. Momma said it best, I had been "one hell of an actress."

No more faking. No more hiding. No more hustling. I just want to be real.

CHAPTER 7

Like Ken and Barbie with a Bible

Entering marriage with 4th grade ideals

Like most little girls, I dreamed of walking down the aisle, wearing a wedding gown, and taking a new last name. I imagined having babies and raising a family in a beautiful home. My dreams began in the fourth grade—in Mrs. Stroud's class, as a matter of fact. As a child, I practiced with my baby dolls. I had one that was so life-like, even her soft plastic head smelled like a newborn baby's. I pretended to have the baby dressed and cooing as I got delicious dinners on the table for my husband who just came in from work. I wore an apron and imagined a spotless home and children who said *yes ma'am* and *no sir*.

I have no idea where these ideals came from, as I was raised in a 1980s blended family by a dad and a stepmom who both worked outside our home. My dad actually handled more domestic duties than my stepmother did because his firefighter shifts allowed him to be home a few evenings a week. My mother didn't model the vintage 1950s image either. She managed everything in her home as well as ran her own restaurants and bars. Nevertheless, even as I entered adulthood, I dreamed of my idyllic future marriage. My husband and I would be just like the Ken and Barbie figures I had also role-played with as a child: beautiful, fabulously dressed, and perfect.

In real life, the roles were perfect, but the people were not. I had groomed myself to play a part, to be someone's other half. I wasn't prepared to be a whole person in a healthy relationship. I didn't know myself, much less the kind of man who would make an ideal companion for me. Rather, I married a man who loved the best version I presented. Only I didn't realize it at the time, and neither did he. We never saw past the roles we would play. We both dreamed of marriage and family. So, I at 25, and he at 33, just took what seemed to be the next logical step; we got married. I suppose he was doing all the things he believed he was supposed to do, too.

I wasn't looking at who he was as a person, so much as who he would be to me, and I to him. We were young and had immature ideas of love and marriage. I, for one, did us both a disservice when I considered our roles in marriage apart from our personalities, character, and dreams as individuals. We started our marriage off with obstacles I never even saw, like not really knowing who I was or what purpose I wanted to fulfill in life *for myself.* My thinking was limited to who I would be to someone else: wife and mother. Furthermore, I didn't understand the reciprocal nature of love at all. I believed love was earned by doing good things. So I did good things, and to an extent that made me a very good wife. I believed that as long as I gave of myself, he would continue to love me and approve of me—and for a long time, he did. But, I regret that. I regret that I started our marriage out that way.

Like any immature lover, I enjoyed the feelings of being adored and accepted. We had a first-date love, the kind where you put on your best dress and fix your hair just right. I laughed at all his jokes and used the right fork. I smiled all the time and deferred to whatever he suggested. First date lovers keep their opinions, flaws, and secrets to themselves. I did that the entire 15 years we were together. Sadly, I didn't realize I was doing anything wrong. I thought this was how good wives carried themselves inside and outside of their homes. I lived out my fourth grade ideal in my Barbie Dream House with Ken and our two Barbie babies.

The "Ladies of Grace"

Clearly, leading up to our marriage, my ideas of being a good wife were already skewed. The Ladies of Grace only added fuel to the fire. Just before our wedding, the ladies group at our church hosted a series of Sunday morning classes on being a godly wife. I was strongly encouraged by the Pastor's wife to attend, so naturally I did. They were kind, Christian women, and I believe they meant well. As a perfectionist though, I swallowed every morsel of their advice like it was manna from Heaven.

I learned that it was my duty to look good for my husband at all times, to have my hair styled and my makeup on, to smell good, to dress nicely, and to make myself available to him sexually at any time. A good wife never wears her husband's t-shirts to bed. She makes his coffee and prepares his meals, keeps an immaculate home, and raises beautiful, obedient children. She doesn't allow the children to annoy him when he comes in the door from a hard day at work. She busies herself in the kitchen making dinner while allowing him to rest and have some leisure time to disconnect from his stressful job. A godly wife carries herself well in public and defers to her husband's opinions, whether publicly or privately. She doesn't burden her husband with her problems; that's what her friends are for. There was very little mention of a modern family with a working wife, her roles outside of the marriage, or his responsibilities to their relationship. There was no encouragement for a woman to pursue her own interests, dreams, or career. There were no clauses for sickness or exhaustion—just a recipe for a perky wife and happy home, which was exactly what I wanted. In hindsight, it was a formula for function, and ultimately, for failure.

The Ladies described men as caretakers, the wife's covering. They portrayed them as stressed-out, simple-minded, and sex-starved. It was made clear that sex and compliments solve 99% of a man's problems. If a husband was unhappy, he simply needed more sex and more affirmation from his wife. Neither of these are bad. Sex is good. Encouragement is good. But I didn't know then that real men are more than simpletons with insatiable appetites for sex. I hadn't learned that real men are deeper than that. Real men are not impatiently waiting in the recliner for their slippers and scotch. They aren't demanding their chicken dinner at 6:00 PM and obligatory sex after the wife gets his children to bed. And women—women are so much more than functional. But I didn't know that either. I didn't believe I could be both a good wife and mother *and* have dreams and goals, a career, and a mind of my own.

I didn't know that a strong man appreciates and encourages independence in a woman, that a confident man is not intimidated by her strengths. Women can be role models to their children, to other women, and within our communities, not merely the wearers of lace and the wipers of noses. I had learned function though. And a Martha by nature, I set out to do, do, do everything I could to be the beautiful, doting wife to a man who attended the godly husband classes across the hall, where he learned to provide for his family and compliment his wife's chicken dinner. The principles we learned were not all bad, but I internalized The Ladies of Grace's instructions as the red-letter gospel for being a good wife.

I outgrew Barbie.

William was the complementary Ken to my Barbie, but twelve years in... I outgrew Barbie. As fake and plastic as my marriage may sound, I was motivated from a genuine heart to have a genuinely good marriage. I desperately wanted to be an exceptional wife and mother. As long as I was able to sustain that image, I felt good about myself. But when I slipped, I felt the sting of failure. Sadly, that's what kept me from reaching out for help when our marriage began showing signs of stress. I was afraid of the inevitable judgment. Besides, until the last months of our marriage, I believed in my husband. I truly believed he would regain control and turn himself around. I didn't want him to be judged. I had faith he would overcome his battle with alcohol. I should have reached out to my Christian friends, family, or pastors for support, but I was scared. I feared William would be judged, and I was terrified of judgment for either of us.

The further my walk has taken me from that marriage, the more I wonder why we were so afraid. Not every church body is this way, nor are its members. In my experience in most of the churches we attended however, I felt tremendous pressure to measure up to some sort of Super-Christian standard. For most of our marriage, in our church circles, we were considered to be lacking in faith if we experienced sickness or disease, or problems in our marriage or with our children. As men and women of faith, especially leadership staff, we were expected to drive well, live well, and wear well. With such unreasonable standards to meet or exceed, whether internally or externally imposed, I never felt comfortable to admit our troubles or flaws. We didn't confront them at church or at home. We hid them, and we pretended everything was as it should be. I wish I had allowed myself more love, more grace, and more vulnerability. Rather, I just kept doing enough right things and avoiding enough wrong things in an effort to prove my worth as a Christian woman. In essence, I lived in pursuit of more gold stars from God and other Christians that would make me feel worthy of love and acceptance.

It's sad. The place I should have felt the most love was from my husband, and the place I should have had the most safety to reach out for help was our church, but those were the places I was most afraid to be real. Instead, I was Barbie with a Bible, the real me hidden under layers of pretty dresses, sparkling accessories, and a leather-bound cover.

I couldn't imagine reaching out for help, so I reached in until our failing marriage ultimately exhausted my limited personal resources. He used up all of my grace, all of my respect, and all of my love. I used up all of my faith, all of my self-worth, and all of my hope. Just as a flame consumes air and fuel until it dies out, we consumed ourselves until there was nothing left. No one can sustain perfection forever, and no one can truly, deeply love an image. I don't blame him, or myself, or the church. It just happened. In hindsight, I know that the isolation I felt was rooted in perfectionism. It prevented me from making myself vulnerable enough to get help and support for either of us, and it finally led to our implosion.

Abandoning 4th grade ideals and leaning into love

Not long after the divorce was final, William seemed to be sober. I was happy for him, especially for the kids. He was present at everything they did. He coached their sports teams. He came to all their school events. In fact, he was there so often, that when we showed up to Open House or Meet the Teacher, most teachers assumed we were married. We were cordial to one another and usually sat together for parent meetings and school performances. The difference after divorce was that, at least for me, it was not for show. I made the effort because regardless how things had ended between us, our children deserved parents who would be present in their lives and work together to make positive decisions for them. When they were with him, he took them places and did things with them. He really seemed to be invested in them. After so many years of his absence during our marriage while he struggled with alcohol, I couldn't ask for more than his presence in their lives. Although William and I didn't see eye to eye on every matter, I genuinely felt like we co-parented together nicely.

No longer plastic

With him sober, and the divorce well behind us, life seemed to be finding a comfortable new rhythm. Several times a week, I either walked the track with Danielle or ran it by myself.

I found reprieve in getting outdoors, clearing my head, and staying fit. Running gave me much needed time to think. One particular evening, over two years after the divorce, I was out running and thinking. Os and I had been dating for some time by then, but we were still taking our relationship very slowly. We hadn't even said those three little words to one another, but I knew those feelings were there for us both. As I ran, I contemplated what it really means to love someone. After all, I had misled myself before. Hell, I had been straight up wrong before. How could I be sure this relationship would be different? I'll never forget where I was on the track when it struck me. It was dark outside, but still hot as I passed under a giant oak tree near the main entrance. Acorns crunching underfoot, I saw the glaring difference, and it stopped me cold.

My feet came to an abrupt halt, and my hands hit my knees. I was falling in love with a man, not with an ideal. I was moved by who he was as a person, and I admired what he stood for. I was physically attracted to him. I wanted to pursue him and be pursued by him. For the first time in my life, I was not enamored with the idea of marriage and having babies, of being a perfect wife and mother. I was not fixated on roles. I was falling in love with *him*.

I've read, "One of the great joys of falling in love is the feeling that the most extraordinary person in the entire world has chosen you."[iii] Ironically, I read it from a book Os had given me for my birthday that year. I was falling in love with someone extraordinary who was falling in love with me. We were taking our time to carefully reveal ourselves to one another, faults and all. We were giving ourselves space to heal from our divorces without pressuring one another to be the healer. We each desired to mend our own wounds, to grow from our own painful experiences.

Divorce did not leave me bitter against men or marriage, but honestly, I still didn't know if I wanted to marry again. It was a risk for us both to keep moving forward in our relationship without having settled that question for myself, but we acknowledged that neither of us had it all figured out. So we agreed to be honest with ourselves and with each other. We graciously afforded one another the space to figure it out along the way—without a plan—while I slipped off my heels of plastic and perfection.

CHAPTER 8

Perfect Parenting

Type A parenting

I had more than plastic Barbie shoes to take off. I had years of parenting ideals to shed as well. Perhaps my affinity for being a perfect mother began when I held my sweet-smelling baby dolls at age eight, or maybe during my pregnancy as I voraciously ingested parenting books and breakfast tacos, or perhaps it was the moment I held my daughter in my arms for the first time. One thing is certain, more than a baby was birthed that morning. There was love. In fact, I was completely consumed with the momma-love. It was tender, and it was fierce.

When the nurse nestled my baby girl in my arms, I kissed her chubby cheeks. With tears, I whispered on her skin, "I love you. Momma loves you." The entire first day in the hospital, I kept examining her little fingers and toes, touching her face and hair, smelling her sweet skin. I thought over and over again, *she's perfect*—not in the sense that she hadn't made any mistakes in her young life yet—but that I hadn't. Now that she's a teenager, I can honestly say, I have messed up plenty of times. I have yelled when I should have hugged. I have controlled when I should have released. I have hurt when I should have healed.

As a first time parent, I did all the things I thought perfect parents do. Before she even arrived, I went to every doctor appointment and sonogram, attended birthing classes, and registered for breastfeeding classes. I decorated her nursery and stocked up on two of everything from Babies R' Us. I quit working my corporate job at a Dallas law firm when I was eight months pregnant because I wanted extra time to prepare to stay home with her. After she was born, I nursed her for a year, pumped incessantly, and got her to every single well-check on time. I dressed her in girly dresses with big bows on her head and had her portraits made every month. I followed a healthy baby feeding plan, and even tried the unthinkable advice (to me at least) of leaving her in her crib to "cry it out" a few times, but I couldn't bear that another minute. It was hard to know what to do when there was at least one theory contradicting every other theory I'd read about parenting, and I was trying so hard to do it perfectly. That's the thing about perfectionism. I believed so strongly that there was singularly a right and a wrong way to do everything that I wouldn't relax, listen to my heart, or trust my own intuition. The more I read, the more overwhelmed I felt that I was doing it all wrong, and I was going to somehow wreck her life. Further, my little angel developed a very independent personality early on, which made my appetite for perfection increasingly harder to satisfy.

It was challenging to be perfect when my five-month-old was scream-crying at Target and my cart was half-full of groceries. I felt like everyone was staring me down while my sweaty palms gripped the cart and my mind raced, *Do I stay? Or do I go? And if I go, can I leave my screaming baby in the cart?* It was even harder to be perfect when my toddler threw herself down in the church parking lot, yanked the perfectly-placed bow out of her hair and threw it to the ground, and refused—I mean *refused*—to stand up. I couldn't just pick her up because not only was she making herself like spaghetti, I was already loaded down with a purse, a diaper bag, her brand-new squirming baby brother, and her wet Elmer's glue-macaroni-glitter-masterpiece that would inevitably end up all over my nice dress. Perfection is too much to ask after I had been up all night with my infant son who cried seven hours straight with double ear-infections and refused to nurse because of his pain. When I came off of a night like that and my two-and-a-half-year-old ray of sunshine boldly announced that she wouldn't be wearing dresses anymore, that alone sent me from a tender request, "Darling, please…" to a clinched-teeth "Put on the freakin' dress."

By the time Reese was three years old, and James was fifteen months, I was coming unraveled. I was so hellbent on raising perfect children that I lost sight of my calling to raise them up to become well-rounded, contributing adults. I couldn't even imagine them as adults yet. They were still in diapers and potty training. Even Kindergarten seemed light years away. At the time, I had no idea how much weight I put into what other people thought of my children, but I did because ultimately I felt my children were a reflection of me. In my mind, every tantrum, every bout of Sunday School separation anxiety, every disheveled or mismatched outfit she put on pointed to a momma who must be doing something wrong. So, I allowed myself to get sucked into every battle or misstep, to narrow my lens so tightly in each moment that I lost sight of the journey as a whole. I needed my children to look good and to be good because I needed them to make me look good. Consequently, I put extreme pressure on my daughter to be perfect. I found myself yelling at her more and more. I couldn't get through books fast enough to learn how to control her, force her to behave properly, and make her be seen and not heard. I was hard on that sweet child until a split second at her bedroom door changed everything.

I nearly crushed my little girl.

Reese was four years old. She stood in her doorway adamantly rebelling against something I had asked her to do. She was probably frustrated about some dress I had asked her to wear or socks I had insisted she match. Regardless of the catalyst, I had reached my boiling point. My exhaustion from child-rearing and my emotional overwhelm from Williams' alcoholism had left me frazzled and angry, and I came down on her hard. I grabbed both of her little arms, and I yelled at her. I was so furious I can't even remember what I said, but I know with certainty it was through a locked jaw.

Her entire countenance shifted in an instant. Reese's big tearful eyes and soft quivering lip arrested me. I can still see that look on her face. It was fear. It would have been easy to keep yelling had she flashed back at me with anger or attitude. But that face...my little girl was afraid of me. *I did that. I just made her fear me.* I stopped. When I released her arms, she cowered away from me. She backed herself down the hallway, crying, and no amount of coaxing or apologizing would reassure her. I slid my back down her doorframe to the floor, dropped my head to my hands, and I cried too. In that instant I knew I was going to crush her free-spirit if I kept trying to make her like me. She would never be perfect. Hell, neither would I.

She eventually came to me and let me hold her. I whispered through my own sobs, "Mommy's sorry," over and over and over again. It's all I could say. My eyes swollen with tears and my heart with incredible remorse, I prayed desperately that night for God to help me. I told Him, "This can't be a slow process of personal growth or weeks of Bible study. I need You to help me *right now*. For Reese. Please God, do this for her. She needs me to be a better momma than this. Please God, do this for her, not me."

My anguish over the fear I had put on my sweet girl's face motivated me to be honest with myself and with God. I wasn't really used to that. I thought I was, but really I judged myself by my good intentions, and I told God what I thought He needed to hear. I had been filtering my prayers through what I wanted Him to see. I know that's crazy, but it's how I prayed…with so much scripture and good intention that I never acknowledged actual problems. I preferred to speak the solution to God and tell Him how I was going to fix things.

I honestly believe that was the first time in my life that I sensed that perfectionism wasn't absolute. It wasn't leading me safely down the path of the sweet little life I had imagined. Something was not right here. Ascribing to all the expert advice was not making me a perfect mother or her a perfect child. Following the rules was not producing the results I anticipated. In those moments, I didn't fully understand the hold perfectionism had on me, but I knew that what just happened with my little girl was a result of me believing so strongly that she was a reflection of me that I was trying to force perfection on her, so I would look perfect too. It wasn't about her dress or socks anymore; it never was. It was about how her appearance reflected mine. I had been imposing myself on my daughter because she was threatening my perfect image.

All the times I imagined my white picket fence life, it was absent of problems or challenges. I didn't expect them because by God I was following all the damn rules. I certainly didn't know how to handle them when they came. I was ill-equipped for this. Her frightened face shook me to my core. I loved my sweet girl ardently, but I was crushing her. I knew in that moment that I was the one who needed to change—not her. But I didn't know how.

God did what?

I pressed into my faith in the most genuine way I ever had up to that point in my life. I was outside of my comfort zone and starkly aware that so much more was at stake than my flawless appearance. I needed God to help me be the mother she deserved, even at the risk of judgment or disapproval from others. I wanted to develop a deeper concern for how I could impact her future as a young woman, than how she could impact my present as a young mother.

God honored my little girl, and He honored my sincere, broken pleas. Once I told Him the truth, through prayer He revealed that I should celebrate her personality, not fight it. He showed me how He did it Himself with His son, Adam. It was remarkable, but so subtle I had never noticed this part of the Creation story before. Genesis 2:19 describes what happened after God filled the Earth with all the animals.

Now the LORD God had formed out of the ground all the wild animals and all the birds in the sky. He brought them

to the man to see what he would name them; and whatever
the man called each living creature, that was its name.

He brought the animals to his son to see what he would call them? And then He just rolled with it? Wait. God let *Adam* name the animals? I didn't know that. I just assumed God named them Himself. After all, He made them. What if Adam screwed it up? I mean, he was brand-new on the Earth himself. How would he know what to call them? And if he called them something ridiculous, they would be stuck with those names for eternity, unless God changed them later. (And perfectionists do that.) But, God didn't. *He brought them to the man...and whatever the man called each living creature, that was its name.*

This one verse in the Bible has transformed my approach to parenting more than any book, any class, or any parenting expert ever has. God, the Maker of the Universe, and a Father Himself, released control. Unlike me, He actually is perfect—but, He relaxed. He sat back as a Daddy and watched His son marvel at the animals and give them all names. God demonstrated that He trusted His son to do something very important and lasting.

I didn't want to be a controlling parent. I wanted to do what God did. I wanted to sit back and take in Reese's wonder and her unique way of seeing and doing things. I wanted to celebrate her free-spirit, not crush it or control it. I wanted to observe her and appreciate her. I no longer wanted to make her just like me; I wanted to open myself up to be more like her.

This one statement in Genesis has filtered my responses to her over and over again to this day. Reese has a big, bright, loud personality. Anyone who knows her hears it and sees it. Her conversations are more like presentations where she commands your attention with a song and dance as she unleashes some new information or story from her day. That girl is a one-man band. As a recovering perfectionist, I won't lie, she can be incredibly challenging to parent at times because she's not concerned about perfection at all. She's free. That one word from God changed the trajectory of our relationship, and more importantly of her entire life. She will never be a perfect kid, but she is going to be one hell of a woman. I'm going to sit back and watch her do it.

Doing it all myself

Since that night with my precious daughter, I've done plenty of holding on tight and letting go. There's a lot of juggling personalities in our house, and she and I have both learned to appreciate each other's temperaments. She would prefer to bounce from room to room leaving empty cups and candy wrappers, shoes and socks, and books in her wake. It never seems to bother her in the slightest. I, on the other hand, am doing breathing exercises to avoid the inevitable heart attack from just looking at all the clutter she has left behind in the first five minutes she comes through the door. Naturally, as a means of personal survival, I spent years coming along behind her picking stuff up because she is messy, and I am not. She is all over the map, and I am on a mission. She is an explosion of sound and stuff, and I am a first responder tidying up. It worked quite nicely for us both until I realized I was not really parenting anymore; I was taking care of my needs again. That—and I was exhausted from doing it all myself.

As a kid, I was responsible for taking care of my own things and doing chores around the house as a contributing member of our family. My dad taught me how to wash dishes, fold laundry, clean my own room, vacuum, dust, wipe down baseboards, mow the lawn, wash cars, and start dinner. We were all expected to do these things. In junior high, I had already accrued enough basic life skills to take care of myself—at least for a little while. I was taught by example to save money, take care of my responsibilities before I enjoyed my privileges, and most certainly to respect authority. I still say *yes ma'am* and *no sir*. My parents didn't apologize when they asked us to vacuum the floor or fold washcloths. We were members of a family in which we were expected to contribute. I want to teach my children these same values and skills. It's not always easy as a perfectionist though. It's easier to just do it myself.

I'm faster. I like my way of doing things. It only takes me one time. And the kids never complain when I do it all for them. They even say *thank you.* But there's a cost to doing it all: It's exhausting to me, and it's a disservice to them. Sometimes I tell myself, *but they work hard all day at school, and they have additional schoolwork when they get home. I don't want them to*

Andria Flores

have to do things around the house after all of that is done. I want them to go play in the afternoon sun like kids are supposed to do. But what message am I sending them if they aren't expected to contribute to our family? After all, I work hard all day too, and I have plenty more to do once everyone gets home. I can't just not make dinner, not pay bills, or not do laundry...right?

When I left William, Reese was eight years old and James was six. They were at ages when they could have been learning to do more chores around the house. But between new visitation schedules, increased stress levels, and my hefty divorce-guilt, I delayed teaching them basic skills. It took a couple of years of recovering from all of that before I began asking them to do more to contribute. I realized it wasn't benefitting them when I did it all for them. When I expect them to pitch in, I'm not robbing them of playtime; I am investing in their character and life skills.

I think I realized I was allowing divorce-guilt and perfectionism to stunt my children's development in terms of managing their responsibilities when my daughter proudly announced the first week of fourth grade that parents are no longer requested to sign off on their daily planners in their school binders. *Well how am I supposed to know if she's doing her work? [really long pause] Oh. That's her responsibility. Her teacher will hold her accountable.* I began to wonder what else I might be micromanaging for them. In what other areas was I still treating Reese like the second grader and James like the Pre-K'er they were when their dad and I divorced? A lot had changed in two years. They had grown up significantly, but I was still treating them as if they were little. So I began having them pick up their own dishes, help me dust, vacuum, or wipe down countertops, and make their rooms tidy each night.

When I think back on the responsibilities I had during my childhood, I also remember riding my bike all over the neighborhood, playing with our dog Casper in the backyard, roller skating on the driveway with my George Michael cassette turned up until it was distorted, playing "house" and "school" and Barbies, having sleepovers with Danielle, playing Atari and watching Gilligan's Island. I played a lot—after schoolwork and chores were done. It wasn't so bad. My kids can do that too. We all benefit when we contribute to our family and home, and we all suffer when we don't.

How do I teach my kids to foster their own self-worth?

When Daddy stapled my awards to the kitchen wall or looked over my report cards, he would say, "I'm so proud of you." I lit up. I loved to make my daddy proud. I never saw anything unusual about that. I think most of us want to make our parents proud, even as adults. So when I became a parent myself, I raised an eyebrow the first time I read that we should temper how often we tell our children we are proud of them. *What? No, I want them to know how proud I am when they have done something well.* So I told them the same thing my daddy told me.

One day however, it clicked for me. I heard it in their language. "Mommy, look what I did!" "Hey Mom, did you see my report card?" And "Mom, watch me!" a gazillion times in a row. James and Reese loved to see me happy. They've always liked pleasing me. It's actually something I used to aim for when they were toddlers, but something about it feels unnatural to me now. It turns out that the more I transferred my own self-worth from what others thought of me to what I thought of myself, the more cognizant I became about where I heard my children placing their self-worth. They were looking to me to see how they should feel about themselves.

When James commanded my attention, I looked and applauded his stunts off the top of the slide at the park. I gave attention to and cheered Reese's dance routine to the latest funky pop song. I wanted them to know, "I see you. I am proud of you." So like my daddy, I told them so. But now, more than that, I want them to be proud of themselves. When Reese cleans her own room, or when James organizes his Legos, I want them to engender a sense of pride in themselves. When Reese receives an "A" on her science test, I want her to feel good about the work she put into it. When James scores a goal or overcomes an obstacle at school, I want him to recognize the effort he and his teachers or coaches invested.

I want to teach my kids to own what's theirs—successes and failures. Most of my life, I avoided failure as often as I could, and I deflected it when it landed in my lap. But I've since learned there's value in gracefully owning my proud moments as well as my shameful ones. As a controlling, perfectionist momma, I hadn't left them any margin for mistakes, and I owned everything for them. I felt like a failure when they fell short, and I felt like mom-of-the-year when the achieved and excelled. Not anymore, at least not like that.

Of course I feel proud of them or disappointed in them, and I do express that. But, I temper my responses. I no longer own their moments for them. I point them back to themselves. "I bet you are so proud of yourself." Or, "How does that make you feel?" Or, "Look what you did!" When I give James and Reese freedom to make mistakes within the boundaries of what is expected and appropriate credit for whatever they have done—good or bad—I give them the gifts of ownership, acceptance, and self-worth. I teach them to value themselves and others, not to simply strive to meet someone else's expectations, even their mother's. I want my kids to do something I didn't do much of—think for themselves.

Parenting for the approval of others

It took several scenes from church parking lots and Target grocery store aisles—and encouragement from other moms like Carla—before I learned it really doesn't matter what other people think my kids need. It's my responsibility to raise them. Further, as a single parent, I've also learned that as much as I'd like for my ex-husband and me to raise our children with the same values, principles, and guidelines, we are running two separate households now.

The first year or two after our divorce, I worked diligently to try to sync our parenting styles and household rules and expectations. As a people-pleaser, I used to filter my parenting decisions and discipline techniques through my need for his approval. Even though I wasn't married to him anymore, we still parented our children together, and I wanted to maintain consistency for them and some sense of approval from him. I finally had to let that go. I learned to recognize and trust my own instincts and to develop and support my own values—even when they differed from his.

I went through a long period of time when I tried to convince him what the kids needed from us as parents. I worked hard to present a unified front to them with regard to principles and values. For example, I struggled initially that he spent so much more money on gifts at Christmas and birthdays, on name-brands, and electronics. Not only did I not have the same financial resources, I came to respect that neither did I share the same financial principles and values. Regardless of my budget, I never wanted to spend that kind of money on gifts and the-latest-and-greatest anyway. I had to embrace the fact that he is well within his rights as an adult and as their father to make choices for his own household, whether they align with my values or not. He may hand them a $600 iPhone, and I may require them to pay a portion of it monthly. As a recovering perfectionist, it meant I had to let go of trying to control or convince William how to parent. That's not my responsibility. Though growing up in two households is never ideal, our children are smart enough and adaptable enough to navigate the differences between two homes and parenting-styles.

Parenting for the approval of my kids

Finally, I've learned that I am not parenting for the approval of my kids. This can be a hard one at times because divorce-guilt never completely goes away. At least it hasn't for me yet. I hate that they have to transfer their belongings between two houses twice a week. I hate that they say, "your house" or "dad's house" instead of "my house." I never hear my kids say to their friends, "Can you come to my house?" Everyone should have a singular place that feels like home. My only prayer is that these hardships will make them stronger and more empathetic children, and ultimately, adults.

I've learned to pick my battles with them, rather than pick them apart. I can allow James to stuff his clothes in his drawers rather than hanging them or folding them. After all, he's the one who's wearing wrinkles, not his OCD mother. I can allow Reese the freedom to wear mismatched clothes or be messy and loud because that's who she is. And when she begins to hedge at disrespecting me, I let her know she's crossing a line, and she honors me. I don't want my children to be quiet, or perfect, or afraid. I want them to be real, and messy, and brave.

It's not always easy, but I've come to believe that parenting does not have to be exclusive of friendship or authority. We can maintain both, if we seek balance and honor boundaries. The boundaries get tested most by Reese. Her nature is to ask lots of questions, and she is bold about it. But once I understood that it's not my responsibility to answer every one of her questions about divorce, I am now happy to explain what I can and certainly what is appropriate without slipping into a position to tell all or to defend myself. When she first became aware that I might be dating someone, she asked lots of questions about that too. But I was able to hold her off for over two years before I introduced her and James to Os and his children. Back then, she liked a boy, so it felt appropriate at that stage of our recovery to let her know I liked one too. Two years later, I finally introduced them to the man in my life.

Having boundaries with my children has been good for all of us. Reese has developed her own sense of when to push and when to refrain. James, on the other hand, doesn't push too hard. But as he matures, I see him forming boundaries of his own. He doesn't want me to hold his hand in public anymore. He absolutely does not want me to see him cry. My sweet little boy is exercising his own independence, and I let him have that because I respect him and his boundaries. As a recovering perfectionist, learning to relax as a mother has meant becoming comfortable with releasing control when I can, and taking a firm stand when it's warranted, even at the risk of being unpopular with my children.

I am not a perfect parent, but I am a damn good momma. My kids are not perfect, but for me to expect anything different isn't a reflection of their flaws, it's revealing of mine. If I were to continue imposing my perfectionism on my children, I would condition them toward self-loathing rather than self-worth because they would never be able to meet my unreasonable standards, much the way I could never meet my own. If I continued down that path, I would stifle our relationships. I would lose sight of my mission to launch healthy, confident adults because I'd remain so focused on corralling perfect little children. There's been a shift at our house. We aim to give one another our very best, and we offer one another simple grace when we get it all wrong. It means nobody has to be perfect anymore. Instead, we acknowledge and embrace our imperfections.

Andria Flores

CHAPTER 9

The Safety Net of Friends

What if I lose my little girl? What if she loses me?

Perfectionism didn't just affect the relationships inside my home, it affected the relationships outside my home as well. I love people deeply, but I haven't always had deep friendships. Without realizing it, I made it hard for people to connect with me through my tall fences and closed gates. During my marriage especially, I didn't take risks to confide in friends or to reach out for help when I needed it because I thought that meant I was weak. Rather, I defaulted to what always seemed safer: handling things myself.

In October 2009, my little girl suddenly fell ill with the swine flu. She was in Kindergarten, and the media was reporting daily about children who were dying from this strain of the flu. People were wearing masks in public and on airplanes. The day Reese was diagnosed, I had just watched a story documenting a local family who had suddenly lost their little girl to the illness. The child, barely older than my daughter, was out riding her bicycle one afternoon, then fell so ill by evening that she died in her sleep that night. So for a week, while Reese was sick, I slept in her bed every night so I could listen to her breathe. Naturally, I didn't sleep much, which gave me time to not only worry about her, but to ponder my own fate as well. Just two weeks prior, I had detected two small lumps in my left breast.

I had been to my doctor, who sent me to have a mammogram, who asked a second doctor to perform a sonogram on my breast. I attended those appointments by myself. I told William about the lumps when I found them, and I shared the doctor's findings with him as well, but he never joined me on the visits. He didn't do well in the face of physical ailments. I think he struggled to acknowledge sickness or disease because he couldn't reconcile it with his faith. We were taught at church that we had dominion over our bodies, therefore if we became sick or diseased, it was a direct indication of our lack of faith. Academically, I understood it to mean that God is perfect and faithful, and I

120   Andria Flores

am not, so being sick is my fault. But spiritually, that reasoning never made sense to me. I couldn't understand how sickness pointed to sin or a lack of faith. After all, was my little girl sick because she somehow brought this on herself? Of course not.

It really frightened me when they scheduled me to come back again in two days for a biopsy. The nurses assured me it was a quick and painless procedure. It was, but I went to that appointment alone too, and that hurt. At the same time, something about doing it alone also made me feel strong. Reese and I were not well, William disconnected from us, and I didn't reach out to anyone else. I decided I was strong enough to handle it on my own. So, I brushed my little girl's damp hair back from her hot forehead while she slept, and I wondered what would happen to her and her little brother if I were diagnosed with breast cancer. I muffled heavy sobs into her pillows so I wouldn't wake her. I was scared, but I tried not to completely surrender to the thoughts of either of our mortalities.

Perfectionism isolated me from comfort, from humanity, from the depths of emotion I wanted to lean into, but strongly resisted. Anytime it began to feel too painful, I retreated to more neutral emotions and practical reasoning.

My husband wasn't dealing with it, and I wasn't dealing with it well. I never gave my friends or family a chance. I didn't really know how. Unaware of how to safely reach out and be seen, I hid. Not only did I hide my fears and my health concerns, but I also took pride in the fact that I could manage this on my own. I convinced myself I had inner-strength for handling my baby girl's night sweats and coughs, and my mammograms and biopsies all by myself. Three weeks transpired from the time I found the lumps until the phone call came with the biopsy results. For three weeks, I wondered if I'd finish raising my little girl and boy. I wondered if I'd lose my long blonde hair. I wondered if I'd die young. In the middle of all of that, I wondered if my precious daughter would pull through the swine flu. They were three of the most uncertain weeks of my life.

If you never take a risk, you don't need a net.

I needed support, but I wouldn't let anyone know. Once my daughter was well and the biopsy reports indicated the lumps were benign, I took my friend, Mia, aside and told her everything. I was so relieved, and I was proud of myself for coming through those weeks on my own. I think I wanted her to see how strong I was, but instead she was offended. Honestly, her response completely caught me off guard. She couldn't believe I hadn't shared my health scare with her as it was happening. She questioned what kind of friends we could possibly be if I wouldn't confide something like that to her, if I wouldn't let her be there for me. Mia was absolutely right, but I didn't get it. I never shared things like that with friends because I never allowed anyone to get that close. I didn't know how to confide in someone like that. I didn't even understand the value of it. I didn't relate connection to comfort. I related it to compromise. In my limited view, connection only created a crack in the dam that held back my all of my emotions.

Maybe I should have reached out to my family. They would have been there for me had I asked. It's an interesting thing about my family…most of them would give you the shirt off their back. But I always felt we were sort of a "live, and let live" kind of bunch. No one usually gets into anyone else's business unless invited. I didn't reach out to them when my daughter and I were sick. I shouldered it myself. I hurt, and I wrestled with wanting to be seen and comforted, but not at the risk of being fragile and vulnerable. I hated to need. It felt like weakness to me, and sucking it up made me feel strong.

Looking back, I regret that I did it alone. Perfection—the idea that I had to keep it all together, all the time—isolated me from connection, something I was designed for, yet somehow disdained. It would be years before I finally understood the power and freedom of vulnerability and the strength that comes from connecting with another human soul. It wasn't until three years later, when I went through my divorce, that my relationship with Carla blossomed right in the middle of my failure and weakness, or that my mother stood by my side and helped me get back on my feet. It's because I let them in though. Ironically, it was at that same time in my life when I shared the news of my divorce with Mia, that I was chastised for abandoning my husband, ruining my marriage, and destroying my children's lives.

Perfectionism stunted my relationships. It kept me bound in fear of being seen for who I really was—although, that became something I craved more and more. Though I felt unseen, I didn't immediately identify myself as the root of the problem. Instead, I resented. I resented my husband for being absent and an alcoholic. I resented Mia for not seeing me as courageous for handling everything on my own. But I was the one holding my guard up so high. I didn't feel safe with the closest people in my life, so I kept my feelings stuffed down deep and pretended everything was fine. But the fact remains, I kept people from seeing me more than I was actually being overlooked.

Since I was a child, I was frequently commended for being mature for my age, but this was one area in which I had never developed. I didn't know how to be vulnerable. I didn't learn how to share what I considered "negative" emotions. In fact, I trained myself not to even feel them. I perceived that disappointment, anger, fear, crying, or confusion indicated a personal deficiency. So I learned to stifle those feelings, to numb them, or to escape them. I busied myself with tasks or other people's problems in order to avoid my own.

William used to praise me for being so emotionally steady and even-keeled, which just affirmed my way of dealing with things on my own. During our marriage, I once heard a well-known minister publicly applaud his wife for being so constant. He said he respected her so much because she was never moved by emotion. I sought to emulate that, and I became so good at it, I controlled my positive emotions too. I learned to be content, but not too happy. I learned to care for others, but not get emotionally attached. I learned to feel strongly about a cause, but not take action for or against it. I trained myself to remain neutral in order to avoid emotional risks. And I was incredibly skilled at it.

I did the same thing when faced with William's alcoholism and the impacts it made on our marriage and children. I was very emotional about what was happening in our home. I cried all the time—in private. I refused to reach out for help. I protected him, and I protected myself from being seen, from being vulnerable, from perhaps connecting with someone who could have helped us. I prayed daily for change, but I never let anyone see me broken. I rarely even confronted William about how I felt because I chose to keep my emotions contained. It was unhealthy for me, and a detriment to my relationships.

A new way to handle problems

About a year and a half passed after our divorce when William started missing visitations with our children. He would text to say he was sick and needed me to keep the kids a few more days. A few months later, Reese mentioned scrubbing a wine stain from the off-white carpet in William's bedroom. I called him late one evening to discuss a school matter regarding one of our children, and he seemed disoriented and hard of hearing, common when he was drinking. There weren't any major incidents at that point, but several familiar signs. It grieved me to my core to imagine my daughter and son learning to enable their daddy like I once had. I broke my pattern to cover and conceal, and I asked the kids a few questions. To that point, they didn't know why we had divorced. They were too young at the time to understand that his behaviors pointed to alcoholism, and I didn't explain it to them.

But now that I was seeing familiar signs, I started asking them questions. I inquired about cleaning the carpet and about Daddy being sick so frequently. For the first time, I expressed to my children that I thought their dad might be drinking. I sensed the need to create a safe place, an open door for them to come to me if something seemed off. As much as I wanted to shield Reese and James from seeing their daddy that way, my greater loyalties were to protect them. Opening up those conversations was uncomfortable and difficult, but a step I knew was necessary for their wellbeing.

Learning to connect

As I continue to move away from perfectionism and toward authenticity, I find that my ability to own my mistakes and shortcomings has, quite frankly, made me relax. Once I acknowledge my own flaws, I'm not nearly as consumed with what others think of me. In fact, I've come to realize that most of the time, they are not. Even when I am judged now, I've usually already acknowledged my missteps to myself, so I'm rarely hurt by other people's opinions anymore. People's judgments, or my perceptions of their judgments, lose their sting when I no longer obsess over what they think.

When I'm not wondering what others may be thinking, or comparing myself to real or imagined standards, I can exhale. My mind quits humming with all those damn voices making me work so hard on myself. I am fully present at dinner, completely engaged in conversation, and entirely aware of the beauty or the chaos around me. I hear and see things I had missed before because I'm getting out of my own head and into the present. I am touched by others' stories and plights. I celebrate their joys and triumphs. I laugh too loud, I cry spontaneously, and sometimes I misunderstand. But I'm not afraid to lean into my emotions anymore. And believe me, I've got feeeeelings!

When I let go of perfectionism, I go to bed at night knowing I truly lived that day. I got outside of myself and connected with people. Connection requires vulnerability. It takes far more courage to be raw and transparent than it does to bookend my days between perfection and people-pleasing. I can fail, say the wrong thing, show emotion, or cry, and I don't have to hide or explain myself. I no longer feel as if I need to suck it up and handle everything on my own. I can be real and brave, not perfectly processed and closed off. It feels natural and authentic.

I remember one of the dates I had with Os in the first two or three months we were seeing each other. He was making dinner for me at his apartment. He invited me to sit down at his bar and pour our wine while he finished preparing our dinner. I liked watching him squeeze the limes and chop the mango for the fresh salsa he was making for our salmon. I was chatting away about something, and when I paused to take a breath, he grinned and looked at me from the sides of his eyes and said, "I love it when you talk to me."

I laughed politely, but I wondered if it were true. I had always been given a hard time in my family for talking too much, especially by William. I suddenly felt self-conscious and secretly questioned Os' motives for saying that to me. He was warm and genuine, and I constantly found myself so relaxed with him that I would chat freely. I also found that he would talk a lot too—and I loved that! Talking, communicating, sharing our hearts has actually become one of the guideposts of our relationship. I cry in front of him anytime the tears begin to swell, which turns out to be quite often. I have a lot of feelings, and I let him see them all. I let him see me angry, or hurting, or afraid. I let him see me puzzled or confused. I let him see me silly, and giddy, and all undone. Os sees me for the beautiful mess that I am, and I have never felt more loved and respected in my life. It takes far more strength to be vulnerable than it does to be stoic and steady. But the risks are so worth the warmth and connection I receive in return.

The safety net of friends

I used to be like a trapeze artist. In fact I was the lead, the seasoned, strong man who starts and finishes the show, but somehow in the nature of his function fades into the background and becomes unseen. You know, the guy with all the muscles who holds on tightly to each performer until he releases them to do some amazing feat. He is the spotter, the catcher. They grab hold of him, depend on him, put their lives in his hands. It is seldom his job to be in the spotlight. He is in the shadows, functioning, playing a supporting role to everyone else. He remains in control and never lets go. But every once in a while, during the finale, another performer becomes the spotter, and he lets go. He depends on someone else's strength to hold him as he does something magnificent in the spotlight. And just like that, he is seen.

I used to pride myself in always being the one who is depended upon, to the degree that it became my comfort zone. I made it my role to keep everything together—especially myself. It was frightening to peel my fingers off the bar and trust someone else to be there to catch me, but I finally got brave enough to let go. After decades of keeping up appearances and protecting myself from truly being seen, I let go. I let go of the impossible standards I held myself to, and I let a few very special people into the deepest parts of my life. Mom, Carla, and Os—they have become my spotters and my safety net. When I feel myself slipping, they are there to grasp my hands in mid-air, or catch me when I fall hard. It is beautiful, though rarely comfortable. Still, I challenge myself to let go, I dare to fly, and I'm cautious about the falls.

Letting people in means they see me when I don't have all my stuff together, and I hate that. But when my closest friends listen to me, help me sort it out, and love me the same without criticism or judgment, they are my very safe place to land, and I love that. There is a sweet exchange.

We are there for each other. I have the most intimate friendships I have ever had in my life. There's no pressure anymore to always be the one who is strong, to hold on tight, to be functional, have it all together, or to always be on. It was an illusion anyway. Real strength came when I learned to let go of the damn bar. Only then could I exhale. Now, I can be vulnerable, I can take risks, and I can be safe because I am no longer working without a net.

A renewed sense of community

Shortly after my divorce was final in March of 2013, I invited my newly formed safety net of friends to a local winery to spend an evening with me. I prepared in advance to tell each of them what they had come to mean to me while I was walking through one of the most difficult times in my life. I invited Danielle, who has known me since the second grade. I invited Carla, who I knew for 14 years before I finally made myself transparent to her. I invited Wes, whom I had come to know over the past year professionally and who was willing to take risks on me and invest in my personal growth. And I invited Os, whom I had been getting to know over the last several months and in whom I was finding the hope of a forever friend.

I shared with them, my sweet community of support, the impact each of them was making on my life. I compared them to the buttons on a remote control. Danielle is my "play button." I can always laugh and have fun with Danielle. I love her free-spirit, and she inspires me to relax. Carla is my "rewind button." She is someone with whom I can reflect and ponder the meaning of life and love, frame by frame. Wes is my "fast forward button." He never stops or slows down, and by association, he challenges me to keep advancing, learn new things, and professionally push the envelope in any way I can. And Os is my "pause button." When I am with Os, life slows between us. I enjoy being in the moment with him. I feel fully present with him, and he with me.

I learned that I need people, and they need me, and that as a community we are strong—like a safety net—not weak. I never really wanted isolation. I longed for connection, but I used isolation as a barrier to protect myself. In all my efforts to be an amazing, perfect woman who people would admire and accept and relate to, I became plastic. How ironic that the connection I longed for required the accessibility I feared. Until my fences started coming down around me, I never really understood the full experience of community. No longer closed off and afraid, I challenged myself to engage in relationships, which has had a profound effect on the course of my life. A couple of years later, it led me to connect with a handful of other beautiful, strong women I unexpectedly came to know at a dinner party.

In August of 2015, Carla told me she'd like to celebrate her upcoming birthday with her closest circle of girlfriends. She gave me their phone numbers, and I texted them all the details of where we'd meet at a local wine café she had selected. In lieu of gifts, one of her friends suggested we each bring Carla a card telling her what she means to us, and that the six of us go around the table toasting her for her birthday with a sincere sentiment or humorous story about her.

Six women, most of us strangers or acquaintances, met together to celebrate our mutual friend. It was rich and energizing. We leaned into vulnerability and expressed deep love and affection to our friend who had made an indelible impact on each of our lives. We had no idea she had come prepared to do the same for all of us. She had written something special to each of us, and read her thoughts out loud to us. It was one of those rare experiences when we voiced intimate emotions people don't always express—the words people inadvertently save for hospital rooms and funeral homes, for wedding toasts and airport send-offs. We read Maya Angelou and sipped cocktails. We laughed and cried. The connection was magical. Then, just 16 days later, we were all stunned by what we learned.

Every single one of us were completely speechless to find out Carla was diagnosed with cancer. We were just celebrating her birthday two weeks ago. She looked amazing, not sick, not cancerous. Carla was in just as much shock as we were. But a community had already been formed, a safety net of friends. And it wasn't just the six of us. Within a few short days a network of her family, friends, and hairstyling clients quickly rallied around her. We held her hand. We cleaned her house. We drove her to doctor appointments. We brought her flowers. We attended her daughter's football games. We researched wigs and options to combat hair loss. We brought her mashed potatoes, ginger ale, and hot tea. We watched Super Soul Sundays and napped together on her bed. We styled her hair. We called insurance companies and doctors. We wrote down medications and argued about the dosage. We ugly-cried and cursed all the shitty things that cancer brings. We prayed.

We walked through dark places with Carla, and we came out still holding hands.

Almost everyone laid in bed with Carla during that time. She wanted us there. It became a thing, being in bed with Carla. It was her safe haven for human connection, physical rest, and emotional release. In the middle of her personal storm, being in bed with Carla somehow offered all of us refuge to feel our powerful emotions too. Lying in bed with Reese six years prior, I was a stoic soldier. I had convinced myself I was strong and brave for shouldering swine flu and a breast biopsy all by myself. No more. Now I held my best friend's hand, got under her covers, and watched Oprah interview Brené Brown, Tim Storey, Glennon Doyle Melton, and Thich Nhat Hanh. Now I talked about fear and death and God out loud. Now I connected with all of my being and held fast to the first friend I had ever truly opened my heart to.

I thank God for bringing me out of a place of fear and disconnection so I could fully experience hard things with my closest friend. *And God, I thank you for bringing Carla out of cancer.*

CHAPTER 10

What is My Purpose?

I wanted to be an astronaut.

I wanted to be one of the first women in space, to be part of missions with teams who discovered things that positively impacted our world. I wanted to make history. From the fourth grade, Mrs. Stroud would pull me out of class to watch Shuttle launches and landings on the TV she had wheeled into her classroom. It didn't matter whose class I was in, all the way through the sixth grade, any one of my teachers would excuse me from class to go down the hall to her room. In junior high, my Honors science teacher, Mrs. Bowden, did the same. Even on an entirely different campus, my teachers still released me to go watch the TV in the science lab. I think they believed in me more than I believed in myself. Mrs. Bowden told me about Space Camp. She said she would write a letter of endorsement for me if I wanted to go. I knew it was very expensive, so I mustered the courage to ask my parents if I could attend Space Camp that summer in Huntsville, AL. I was completely stunned when they said *yes* and made a way to get me there while the rest of my family vacationed nearby. Naturally, I wanted to be the Shuttle Commander, and that's exactly what I was selected to do during our 24-hour mock mission. It was thrilling!

But after a week at camp, I decided I couldn't commit to all the education and training required to become an astronaut because it would interfere with my bigger dream to be a wife and mother. Looking back, that disappoints me, not because I didn't pursue a career in space. I could have done it, but I know now with certainty that it was never my true calling. What saddens me is that by junior high, an archaic paradigm of a woman's role was already informing my life choices. What made me think I had to choose between wife and mother *and* a powerful career? It certainly wasn't the two female role models in my life. My stepmother, with whom I spent the majority of my childhood, was extremely career-oriented. She was a consummate professional, always working or contributing to business women's organizations. She was organized and proficient inside and outside of our home. Further, my mother was an entrepreneur who managed her restaurants and bars successfully. Between the two of them and my dad, I had three role models who demonstrated very strong work ethics, and I watched two ambitious women dedicate themselves to professional success. Still, somehow at 14, I felt I had to choose, maybe because I didn't see how I could perfect all of those roles at once. Whatever the reason, during junior high, I abandoned my lofty dream of becoming an astronaut.

I thought I'd make a good English teacher.

I always enjoyed language, reading, and writing. I had excellent teachers in those subjects who inspired me to advance. I absolutely loved words, the rhythm of stories, the mechanics of sentences, and thanks to my Honors English teacher, Mrs. Stapleton—etymology. By the time I started college, I had decided to major in English Education. Being a natural leader and often a teacher's pet, I reasoned that I would make a great school teacher, and I probably would have, but that wasn't my calling either.

A couple of years into college, I lost interest because I really wasn't passionate about the idea of standing in the front of a classroom year after year. For me, it seemed like a logical choice, a safe one. It didn't occur to me at that point to pursue something else in that field, like becoming a writer. That didn't seem practical. I didn't know any writers. I never even asked anyone about it. So I lost momentum. I continued my college courses for a little while, studied Spanish, and took a few other classes to buy myself time to figure out what I wanted to do. However, I never completed my degree because I lacked the courage to commit to a direction or take a risk on myself. Instead I began working corporately as an executive assistant, and I followed my heart to marry and have children.

I was a damn good executive assistant.

As my college education slowed, I began working in the business world. I spent nearly 15 years as an executive assistant. I already had all the skills I needed to excel. I was organized, detail-oriented, and dedicated. I had writing skills and the discernment to be reserved and discreet. I couldn't have chosen a safer path for myself. I held in high regard the people I worked for, but I was not passionate about the work at all. I valued their approval, which affirmed me more than a paycheck ever could. During the last year or two of my career in that field, I was running out of steam. I often sobbed on my long commute from south Fort Worth to north Dallas because even though I loved who I worked for, I dreaded my job. I was unhappy and unchallenged, but I didn't understand why back then. I only knew I felt professionally unfulfilled. William and I had been married for almost five years when a baby changed everything.

I fulfilled my fantasy of being a wife and mother.

I was elated to find out I was pregnant, and even more excited to find out that with a few financial adjustments, I could quit my job at the end of my pregnancy and stay at home to raise our daughter. William fully supported me in that decision. It's what we both wanted. So I spent the next eight years raising her and her little brother, without thought of ever doing anything else. I loved it! That's one of the greatest losses I grieved when we divorced. My lifestyle as a stay-at-home wife and mom was gone.

Seeking a divorce meant I would have to let go of the one dream that had remained constant in my life. It was an excruciating decision, but one I had to make if I wanted a better life for my children and myself.

I had no idea it would lead me to find my personal purpose, but God knew. God knew the plans He had for my life, even before I was open to them. It wasn't until after I took a step of faith to start my own business in the face of my new single life that I began to see I could experience success apart from supporting someone else's dreams. I realized I could be a good mother *and* have a successful career. It is much safer to hold tight to what is familiar than to lean into faith and let go of familiarity, but dreams are realized in the risk.

I finally knew I was a writer.

In August 2012 I fell in love with a book. It reminded me of everything lovely and soulful inside of me. It gave breath to the words that had been living in my heart and mind for years, unwritten. I relished Anne Morrow Lindbergh's words in *Gift from the Sea*, her own journey of balancing her wifely and motherly roles with her passion to write and to pilot, even her passion to fall in love again. She was the supportive wife of pilot Charles Lindbergh, yet a woman with dreams of her own—and a writer! Her words and her style connected me to my own voice. Once I heard it, I knew. I am a writer.

Much like me, she was a little seeking and a little knowing. She modeled a nurturing spirit and femininity mixed with strength and passion like I had never seen in a woman before. Just reading her words, I felt empowered to be brilliant and amazing. I no longer felt ashamed to be an intelligent, soulful woman. Those attributes suddenly seemed powerful, not small and flighty. She affirmed ideas to me that I already knew in my heart were true. Other times she spoke to me in such fresh and profound ways that I contemplated something from a whole new perspective. It wasn't just her thoughts and perspectives; it was her language. I loved her beautiful imagery and word selections, her soft rolling insights, her confident assertions, and her wit. I thought, *I can write like that.* I almost felt a little arrogant thinking I could write like her, but her voice resonated so deeply within me, I just couldn't deny the power and gifts it was awakening in me.

That's when I discovered my true professional calling. Suddenly, all of my broken little-girl-dreams, all of the *I'm not good enoughs* that prevented me from taking a risk, all of the passion I had dutifully channeled into more practical endeavors, all of the times I had exceeded others' expectations for my life, but fell short of my own...in one weekend, I laid all of those crutches down. I knew: I am a writer. It's not something I am becoming. It isn't a job or career choice, nor is it someone else's dream or expectation for me. It's who I am. It's both fully in me and mine to fulfill.

In the summer of 2012, I immediately began steering my personal and administrative assistant business toward jobs and clients that were either more closely related to the writing industry, or could offer me the opportunity to write or edit in any field. In the meantime, my friend and business associate, Jen, encouraged me to just start writing. I gave her all of the reasons why I couldn't, like not enough time, not enough education, not enough experience. It's like she wasn't listening when she simply responded, "Just start."

Her advice was so simple and straightforward I couldn't successfully dodge it. So, I started. Within weeks, she introduced me to Wes. He was looking for someone to help him write and edit his brand-new leadership blog. I submitted a writing sample, and we met to talk about his vision and mine, to see if we were a good fit. I began working for him about ten hours a week. It was a perfect fit for me with the other clients I had in accounting, social media, and administrative services.

Wes pushed me to learn and grow myself. I began writing and editing for him more and more, and I was able to release other smaller clients. When Wes contracted me to work full-time hours for him, I let my largest accounting client go. Within months of starting my own business, I was working full-time as a writer and editor, primarily on Wes' leadership blog and book projects. He introduced me to a gentleman who has written multiple best-selling books for a well-known and highly regarded leadership expert. This gentleman began mentoring me monthly from out-of-state about the author-writer relationship. He taught me techniques to use while writing for someone else, maintaining the author's voice, and managing our projects.

This was my first experience with a mentor or coach. I'll never forget the first time I met him in person. He came into town for a weekend to help Wes and me get a jumpstart on a book project we were embarking upon. I picked him up at DFW Airport. I felt so intimidated by his success that I dreaded any question he may ask me about my credentials on the drive back to our town. As confident as I felt to work with Wes, I was keenly aware that I didn't even complete my college degree, nor did I have any real experience, save a pitiful little *Lonely Girl Patio Tour* blog, and a few months' experience writing and editing. I thought this man would think what a silly girl I was, but he was kind and generous. Throughout that weekend and the following year, I relished the privilege of his mentorship.

Perfectionism kills creativity.

As a perfectionist, I was achievement-driven and task-oriented, an over-planner and an over-thinker. As a recovering perfectionist, I quickly learned I couldn't be so calculated if I wanted to be creative. I have to be a risk taker, like a kid who nervously scales the high-dive ladder, takes the long walk to the end of the board, closes his eyes, holds his nose, swallows hard and jumps. Until now, I was still gripping the edge of the pool with both hands, just looking up. If I were going to be creative, I was going to have to let go of the edge, climb the ladder, and leap.

As a little girl, there were countless times my dad, or my teachers, would tell me how creative I was. Creativity seemed acceptable as a child. Why in the world did I convince myself I had outgrown creativity? Why did I feel it was no longer valued as a young adult? As I aged, I tightened my grip on practical expectations and released my curiosity for intuition and creativity. Pursuing entrepreneurship with Mom's support gave me the courage to slowly release my fear that I was expected to pursue something practical for myself professionally. Awakening to my dream to write, followed by meeting Wes, added to my confidence to explore my passion. Leaning into risk and creativity put me where I needed to be to climb the ladder and dive in with confidence. **I quit being afraid of being wrong.**

Perfectionism is riddled with fear: fear of failure or making mistakes, fear of what people think, fear of swerving outside the lines. Creativity is a little tousled and undone. Perfectionism is measured and controlled. Creativity says, "Let's finger paint!" Perfectionism says, "No, no, no, because then we'd have to clean it up." *Yeah, I'm a really fun mom.* For years, perfectionism kept me from creating because I feared the messy process. Even now, as a writer, I sometimes fear being unoriginal or uninspiring. I fear the sound of my own voice. I fear being misunderstood—or being understood precisely and being rejected. But then, I remind myself, I don't want to be perfect. I want to be real. Once I began doing it afraid, I stopped being afraid of doing it wrong.

My professional fears stemmed from the same place as any of my other fears: perfectionism. Out of fear, I can whittle a piece I've written down to a small stick if I don't stop editing it. Out of fear, I am capable of worrying so much about what others may think of what I want to express that I will avoid ever writing it. I even fear that perfectionism itself will box me into being common and flat. But I've found two strategies to combat fear. One, I am willing to walk *through* failure. I refuse to let it paralyze me into inaction or indecision anymore. And two, I do it afraid. Once I walked through the flames of divorce, I was no longer afraid to light a match. I survived that humiliation and pain and nakedness. I can certainly handle being edited, rejected, or misunderstood.

I perceived my biggest failure in life to be my failed marriage. The unknowns I faced as a single mother without a job or career path kept me petrified for months. But I kept walking— frightened, crying, failing, insecure—no matter what I felt, I forced myself to keep taking another step. I finally understood that failure and mistakes are an integral part of trying and succeeding. Releasing fear and reaching out in faith to start writing created self-confidence I never had before. I understood that it too would require doing it afraid, not getting it right the first time, and being vulnerable with my work. Now, mistakes don't really rattle me anymore. I take risks and face my fears. And I have finally learned to place more value in what I think of myself than what others do.

The dream and the gifts I needed to write have always been in me. I just needed to get off my seat and dance! I had never taken that step forward because I was too afraid. Without a perfect plan or clear destination, I simply started doing what I presumed writers do. I wrote. I made quality business decisions to pursue my dreams, to develop the raw talents God gave me, and to connect with other people who write. I was still afraid; I just stopped letting fear hold me back. Once again, God revealed to me that He does in fact have a plan for my life. I had not successfully faded into the background like a wallflower at a high school dance. Rather, I just needed to move—and here I am now running toward my destiny. Hell, I'm living it!

Finding faith in myself

I broke old thought patterns and retrained my thinking about my talents, about risk, and about dreams. For most of my life, when I approached anything I wanted to have or achieve, my self-talk prepared me for how I'd feel if I didn't get it. I talked myself out of winning, sometimes out of even trying, because I wanted to prepare myself for the sting of failure and disappointment. It was a self-defeating mind game that made winning seem like a perk and losing, not so bad. Failure both shoved me down and broke my fall.

I'm no longer afraid to put myself out there. Inspired by the simple advice from Jen to "just start," I started writing one piece at a time, sometimes just one paragraph. I started a new blog, *type A plans B*, as a place to publish what I had written. To encourage myself to be seen and read, I entered a writing contest. I won second place for my story about the moment I knew I was a writer. Second place! It felt like a trip to the moon and back. *I guess I didn't need NASA to get me there after all.* I was elated. I don't prepare myself to lose anymore. I prepare myself to win and to achieve. When I win, I am proud that I gave my best. I am genuinely humbled that I was so blessed. I learn from the process. When I lose or fall short of what I let myself work toward and hope for, I am proud that I gave my best, and I learn from the process...usually, more than I learn from winning.

Just two years after winning second place in that contest, I had enough material to begin piecing together the first draft of this book. I entered my introduction into a manuscript contest. Whether placing in the contest or not, each participant was promised professional editorial feedback on their submission. *Really? What did I possibly have to lose?* I entered. I was proud of my introduction. It was not selected for an award, but I received a review from a professional in the industry in each of the two categories I had entered. If you'd have seen me, you'd have thought I just won a yacht or something. I devoured their responses. I weighed what resonated with me and what did not, and I went back to work on my manuscript. My heart overflowed with joy and gratitude. I told everyone about the risk in advance, and I proudly shared the results when they came.

Risk challenges me to be more amazing than sitting still ever did. I refuse to listen to the nagging perfectionist in my head that says I have to get it all figured out before I ever take the first step. Screw that! THAT doesn't work. Risk works. I am taking steps forward in spite of the possibility I'll fail. I thank God I finally started loosening my hold on perfectionism, not as much for the gifts or opportunities that have been opened to me, but for the courage I found to let go. I thank Him for believing in me even when I didn't believe in myself. And I thank Him for being with my children and me, especially during the setbacks.

As I gained momentum in my career, the kids and I were stopped in our tracks at home. The first hard, cold moment came one hot July evening, about two years after the divorce was behind us. I got a call from my nine-year-old son. He had been with his daddy for two days of summer visitation, while Reese had spent the night with a friend. James told me he was hungry. I asked him what he and Daddy were planning for dinner. He said, "I don't know. Daddy has been sleeping since yesterday." James went on to describe how he had made his own breakfast that morning, later discovered the milk was sour, and his stomach hurt. He had been eating Lunchables for two days on his own. He didn't have sheets on his bed. And he was hungry. My heart broke in two when he said he had tried to call me several times, but he finally figured out he had the last digit of my phone number wrong. So, he called each combination until he got it right. The last digit is eight.

James described being on his own for the past two days. He said, "Dad was going to order pizza last night, but he went to bed and forgot." I asked if he would please wake Daddy up so I could talk with him.

William was drunk. This time I did not shrink back.

CHAPTER 11

God is Not Afraid of the F-Bomb

Old problem, new faith

Within thirty minutes of that phone call, I picked up my son and took him out to dinner with Os and me and his two children. William put up resistance over the phone, saying *it* was fine. He told me he had *it* under control and that I was not to come over. But his protests were of zero concern to me. My suspicions over the last several months were confirmed. William was drinking again. I hated what that meant for our kids. In addition to obvious safety concerns, I knew they were seeing a side of their dad they didn't fully remember from our marriage. I know they felt the effects of his drunken behavior before we divorced—his absences, his sullen demeanor, his disconnection from us—but they didn't understand why. When we separated, since I never revealed his drinking problem to them, and he never owned it, they grappled to understand why Mommy left Daddy. So when I picked up James for dinner that night, his dad had him completely convinced that he was just sick. Even though James was the one who had been caring for himself for two days, he felt sorry for his dad.

Within weeks, a pattern was established. William was unreliable and clearly drunk on several occasions when he was scheduled to have our children. In August 2014, I rescheduled my first session with my new writing coach at the very last minute because I had found William drunk when I brought the kids over for their visitation. Weeks later, I cancelled my attendance at a local leadership seminar I was slated to attend and that a client had funded me to go to. The cycle continued over and over again, month after month, that William didn't show up to pick up our children from school, missed visitations because he was "sick," or some variation thereof.

Unlike before, I didn't try to handle it all myself. I did everything I possibly could, then I reached out to my mother and my precious mom-friends when I couldn't be in two places at once. I absolutely couldn't have done it without these women in my life. A year later in August of 2015, I made alternate arrangements for my children with my parents so I could travel to an out-of-state writers conference because I couldn't trust William to have the kids for a few days while I was away. I didn't expose his problems, but I definitely didn't cover for him anymore. I even took him back to court a few times, but in the end, I learned to follow my own instincts first regarding what was best for my children, and I reached out for help when I needed it.

Meanwhile, my sweet children experienced sharp disruptions to their routines and saw their dad in an unusual state. They were devastated and confused. They asked me hard questions. It didn't take Reese long to figure out that her dad was not sick, but drinking. By this time, she was entering the sixth grade and old enough to understand the difference. And just like that, she knew this was a large contributor to Mommy and Daddy's divorce. His familiar behaviors triggered her memory, and it clicked for her. **God parted the sea.**

With God as our Guide, the kids and I came so far in those two to three years following divorce. But prior to the end of my marriage, my spirituality had been stretched. I had been doing all of the things I thought made me a faithful Christian woman, but I needed something more in my faith than obeying all the rules and traditions. I needed relationship.

As the end of my marriage drew near, I gradually abandoned all the preconceived ideas I had been taught about God, and I just talked to Him from my heart, mostly through tears at that point in my life. He answered me. In the empty space that remained after I released all of my religious routines, I found God Himself. Everything else fell down around me, and God was the only thing left standing. Even I was on my knees. It was uncomfortable and unfamiliar, but I openly expressed real need. I dumped it all out before Him and asked, "Am I supposed to stay in my marriage? Or can I go?"

Either answer would require tremendous faith from me. Either path would mean that something in me must be laid to rest. I felt unprepared either way. To this day, no matter how I wrestle with it, I cannot deny that in the face of both faith and failure, God made a way for me. He made a way out of what others would consider my fate: *Marriage anyway. Marriage regardless. Marriage no matter what.* I know God hates divorce. I do, too. Of all the planning I had done in my life, I hadn't planned on divorce. Even when it was staring me down in the last days and hours of our marriage, I didn't plan my divorce. I planned on staying married. So when I actually left, I had no plan B. I had faith and I had fear. And I put all of it in God's hands. I was scared to feel so out of control of my own life during those months. But I was preventing faith from having its own room as long as I held fast to control.

God parted the sea for me. He freed me from that marriage, and He made a way out. There was no way in hell I could have done it without Him. I had nothing figured out. I didn't know what to do next. I was a vulnerable mess. Like Moses and the children of Israel, I fled an oppressive lifestyle I had grown accustomed to. With astonishment I found myself between two walls of raging water. Holding the hands of my frightened children, I looked over my shoulder at one shoreline where fear and failure were chasing me down, threatening to take me back to where they believed I belonged. In those moments, it was hard to leave what was painfully familiar and in some ways falsely safe, but I forced myself to look ahead to the other shoreline.

That's honestly all I could see. Not big plans of rebuilding my life. Not the realization of dreams. Not the Promised Land flowing with milk and honey. Just the shoreline. I had just enough faith to walk the rocky distance between two shorelines. With every fear and insecurity raging on either side, God made a way for me. I had no plan B—hell, no plan at all—but He knew the plans He had for me.

The month of cussing

A spiritual breaking point occurred for me a few months after I left William, which ushered me into what I refer to as The Month of Cussing, or for everyone else, April 2012. A perfect storm for failure in my faith had been brewing. I was struggling to understand the doctrine I had been following, and even ministering, for years. It fed my perfectionism because much of it was laced with rules and conditions and the sense that earning the blessings of God in my life was a product of my faith—and I was an expert at earning rewards and approval. I was doing all the right things, not realizing that faith doesn't require filling up space with doing, or checking off lists, or performing. Rather, faith asks me to be still and make room for mystery and uncertainty. It necessitates margins and invites me to be vulnerable.

For years, I wouldn't let myself bend, much less break, before Him. Even in the intimacy of prayer, I had kept up appearances. I had read about grace, and forgiveness, and the impossibility of being perfect like Jesus. Still I tried to measure up, to perform, and to perfect myself. In so doing, I created a barrier between God and me that kept me from actually experiencing the depths of His grace, the relief of His forgiveness, and the fullness of His love. I could not experience genuine faith so long as I white-knuckled perfectionism. In order to have the kind of relationship with God I longed for, I had to give up control and trying so damned hard to be perfect.

I finally let myself totally break down in front of God. There is one prayer in particular I recorded in my journal with big, scratchy, mean handwriting. It is loaded with F-bombs. I finally allowed myself to feel the anger I had toward my ex-husband for drinking his way through the last half of our marriage. I was completely disheartened that he continued to choose alcohol over us. I was devastated that the life I had longed for as a little girl, and lived as a woman, was now gone. I was pissed off. So I F-bombed my way through all of my pent up hurt and anger and disappointment. And God let me. He didn't edit my prayers or scold me for foul language. He didn't shut me down. He sat back and listened to every last word. Then I heard Him in my heart.

God said, "Finally. Finally, you are telling Me how you really feel. Finally, your prayers aren't neatly packaged between 'Holy Father' and 'In Jesus' Name.' Finally, you trust Me to love you just the way you are. Andria, I don't need you to be perfect, honey. I hear your 'this fucking hurts,' and 'I'm so fucking angry.' It's okay. I can handle it. I see your heart, whether you have the courage to speak it or not. I already know you're angry, and I'm not afraid of your F-bombs. I'm not afraid of your pain or your sin. Keep talking, baby girl. I want to hear you. You don't scare me, honey. I love you. Don't be afraid, I'm not going anywhere."

Holy shit. God is not afraid of the F-bomb. Not that it matters, but I didn't cuss God. I cussed to Him. But I know God gets cussed too. He gets blamed when people have lost a child or a spouse, when they've been diagnosed with cancer, or when they are walking through the darkest times of their lives. Many people do this. Sometimes people turn to God as if He's responsible, then they turn from Him as though He wouldn't understand. I figured out during The Month of Cussing, He is *God.* He can take it, and He does understand. In fact, there is nothing He hasn't seen before. I can't surprise Him, no matter what I've screwed up or how much I've cussed. He saw me hurting—all of me—and He was drawn to me. He wants my authentic self because He loves who I am. And nothing about who I am—no matter how ugly, or snotty, or shameful—will ever scare Him off or make Him turn away.

I had been hiding my tears (and most of my cuss words) from everyone—on my daughter's pillow, at the soccer field, on my knees in the hallway, and behind the wheel of my car. But all this time, He had seen each one. "He kept track of my every toss and turn through sleepless nights. Each tear entered in [His] ledger, each ache written in [His] book."[iv] My head was learning what my heart already knew. I had been hiding nothing from God. Not only did He see me all along, but He was also keeping track of my tears—not a tally of how many times I messed up or failed, as I had supposed, not even how many times I got it right. He was counting my tears. My tossing and turning moved His heart.

It took me some time to truly take that in and understand what it meant. God loves *me*. He loves *who I am*, not how well I perform. He's not cataloging gold stars and blue ribbons. He's not writing me off for yelling at my little girl or divorcing my husband. He's looking at my heart. He's counting my tears. No one counts tears unless they are deeply in love with the one who's crying. I, Andria, am worthy of love. I didn't figure this out in the middle of some shining success. I learned it at the very bottom of my darkest failure. I am wholly loved.

Who am I in Christ? What does that even mean?

Not long after The Month of Cussing, I began seeing a counselor. She challenged me to learn more about who I am in Christ. I had heard that phrase plenty of times in my life, and I loved Jesus. But despite all of my years in church, all of my

Andria Flores

love for Him, and all of my personal study of scripture, I was finding it hard to wrap my head around who I was *in Him*.

Honestly, with no offense to Christ, I wanted to be "enough" on my own. I didn't want to have to identify with a man anymore in order to feel complete. I say this gingerly and with utmost respect because I sincerely honor and revere the Lord. But having made misguided assumptions for the first 37 years of my life that another man's approval made me whole left me broken. In the Southern Bible Belt in which I was born and raised, I still felt the subtle sense that being one man's daughter, then another man's wife, was a sign of validation. So as scared as I was to be on my own, and as much as I loved Jesus, I felt compelled to know and value who I was all by myself.

I had a few conversations with God about this. I expressed that I knew He loved me, but I kind of wanted a little space to figure out who I was on my own. I wanted to see for myself that I could be alright without a man to approve, fix, or lead me. I didn't know how to accept being *in Christ* without taking on that familiar feeling of being subdued, submissive, and small. Jesus is a Man of Faith, not fear, so He didn't seem threatened by my request at all. When I wrestled with who I was and how I fit in with Him, He didn't hold tight with worry or swell up at me in anger. He freely afforded me a safe place to be messy and real, and even wrong. Faith makes room for unknowns, and even failures. God demonstrated His faith in me. As He did with Adam, He sat back to see where I might go with this. I still had conversations with Him, but I relaxed my grip on my guilt for not meeting all of the rules and expectations. I stopped trying to earn His love by doing all the right things. He gave me a safe place to be the unedited version of myself, and in so doing, I found my own sense of value and self-worth.

As I began setting aside old thinking and stellar performances, I felt His quiet, confident love near me. Without judgment, He let me be. He didn't abandon me, and He didn't impose Himself on me. He didn't try to fix me or make me His own. He let me find value in myself. Then, He embraced all that. Without my realizing, He modeled for me how any man should love me and how I should love myself. Wholly. Without measure or conditions, without perfection or performance, I am more than enough. Who I am in Christ is not at all what I thought.

It's not about possession and Him taking ownership of me. I do not belong to Him in the sense that I lose my personal identity. Nor is it about perfection and striving to take on all His flawless qualities. I am not under His thumb so He can control me and make me perfect like He is. Rather, who I am in Christ is about relationship. I am in His heart and on His mind. God thinks about me. He believes in me whether I've got it all together in the moment, or I'm falling apart. He has faith in me, and I in Him. Our relationship is reciprocal. I am His, and He is mine. That's who I am in Christ and Who He is in me.

When my three year old Reese stubbornly sought independence and free-thinking, she didn't want to be herself apart from her momma. She wanted her own identity *and* her momma. But unlike God, I was trying to force her to be "perfect like me." I feared how her behavior might reflect on me. So I bore down and pressed hard for her to fit my perfect image of what a little girl should be like. God does not have that fear. God demonstrated to me personally that He was big enough to give me room to figure out who I was on my own *and* in Him.

As I walked this out in the freedom He offered, I naturally drew closer to Christ, and my spiritual life became less formal. I took my own sweet time finding a new church home, and I no longer prayed to Him as if He was far away tallying my mistakes and successes. When I read my Bible, I discovered others who humbly sought relationship with God, those who dared to seek Him as Friend. David said in Psalms, "As the deer pants for the water, so my soul thirsts after You."[v] God said in Jeremiah, "For I know the plans I have for you…seek me and you shall find me."[vi] David also called God, "…the Lifter of [his] head,"[vii] which tells me it's okay for my head to be down sometimes. And when it is, God cares tenderly for me, gently enough to lift my face back up to His own.

I don't have to be ashamed of feeling tired, sick, discouraged, or afraid. It's part of the human experience. Finding scriptures that resonated my actual feelings of pain or want made me feel alive and authentic. Reading about real relationships gave me a sense of relief about my own imperfections and struggles. I began to approach God in the way I wanted my children to approach me—not with memorized recitations or a tone of entitlement, but with humility, humanity, and warmth, with pure joy and honest pain—with authenticity. *That* felt natural to me.

When William began drinking again a couple of years after our divorce, it doused me headlong into familiar situations, but I no longer felt helpless or afraid to respond. I knew who I was. So, I didn't allow his reactions or fear of other people's perceptions to inform my responses. Rather, I was empowered to protect my children with the fierce love of a momma, a love that doesn't stop to ask permission or concern itself with what others may say.

It saddened me to see his unfortunate turn back to the bottle. Shortly after our divorce, we had established a good co-parenting relationship, the kids were healing, and our lives were moving forward. Ultimately though, watching the effects his alcoholism was having on our children post-divorce affirmed the hard decisions I had made for the kids and myself three years prior. My heart swelled with gratitude that God had faithfully made a way out for us.

Keeping an all-knowing God on a need-to-know basis

As a perfectionist, I had always preferred to keep everything neatly packaged—everything—my purse, my problems, even my prayers. On an intellectual level I knew that God was all-knowing, but I preferred to keep Him on a need-to-know basis. I thanked Him for the good things in my life, and I presented Him with only the problems I had solutions for. It just seemed like the responsible thing to do. I wanted Him to know I had everything under control, and if He had time to help me execute my well-laid plans, that would be great. But if not, I certainly understood He had bigger problems to solve. I didn't want to bother God with my little stuff.

What a gross underestimate of the breadth and depth of God's power. What a limited and distorted perception of God's unconditional and unfailing love. With God, just like every other relationship in my life, I had a complete misunderstanding of what it could be like to be intimate. So I had been giving God the "first-date" version of myself for decades. I wanted Him to see I that was happy and holding it all together. I wouldn't show Him need or want or hurt because I was afraid He would be disappointed in me. I think I knew I couldn't earn His love, but for half of my life, I sure tried.

Authenticity. That's where I found relationship with God. Most certainly, that's where He finally received relationship from me. I am touched by Him, and He is touched by me. Once I dropped the pretenses, He became real and close. The more I come to Him unpolished and imperfect, the more I feel truly seen and accepted. He doesn't love me despite my imperfections, He loves me because of them. I know in my soul that He chuckles at the way I come to Him when I mess up and just tell Him about it in plain talk. Not, "Father God, forgive me for I have sinned." But, "God. [big sigh] God, I really screwed this up. Can you help me?" He responds to me in love. He shows me ways to make things right. I've learned to own my mistakes and failures rather than hide them. I feel safe with God because He already knows all my faults and secrets and never changes the way He feels about me.

We are all icebergs.

My deepening relationship with God sustained me through the hardest times of my life: the months when my failed marriage became public, when I felt painfully vulnerable and exposed, when I was shamed by some of my closest friends for my choice to leave William, when I was scolded for destroying my children's lives, and when I consoled them in their own devastation and grief.

Like anyone, I have felt judged by the tip of my life seen jutting out of the water—by our couple friends, by my ex-husband, even by my innocent children who saw Mommy leave but didn't understand why. It didn't make me angry with those who judged me. It opened my eyes, particularly as a Christian, how I too have made assumptions, thought I understood, or outright passed judgment on others for the tip of their icebergs that I could see in plain view.

We don't see each other's massive block of ice under the surface. We never really know what is going on in someone else's heart or life, yet without thought we sum them up by what we perceive. I am flawed. My children are flawed. My friends and family are flawed. My ex-husband is flawed. Underneath the surface, everyone has struggles, pains, and terrible regrets that aren't for everyone else to see, but they are there. We are all icebergs, perhaps of different sizes, perhaps shaped by different forces and pressures, but we are all fractured by imperfections that are both seen and unseen.

My ice is not better than anyone else's, and I won't pretend it so anymore. Nor will I judge myself, or anyone else, by the portion that juts above the surface. God sees and judges our hearts, which are unseen by man. God is my Judge. I give that power only to Him now, and to no one else. I choose to let go of judgment, whether real or perceived. Instead, I commit to embrace compassion, faith, and authenticity.

God parted the sea for me. He counted my tears. He gave me room to breathe, to figure out who I am in Him, to acknowledge my mistakes and own them. God didn't take away my pain or challenges; He helped me navigate them. I was never alone. When I needed direction, He had plans for me already in place. And when I came to Him vulnerably, God let me stand on His feet and hold His hands like a little girl learning a new dance.

God is perfect, but He is not a perfectionist.

God does not startle in the face of our mistakes, nor does He tremble at our failures. I never once rattled God. I guess none of us can. As much as He wants the best for me, He never promised me a perfect life, nor expected me to live up to unreasonable expectations. I wasn't meant to be perfect. I was meant to be authentic—to have a relationship with Him, with others, and with myself.

As far back as the Garden of Eden, with the very first of us, He anticipated that we were going to get it wrong. So from the very beginning, He created provision in His plans for our mistakes and imperfections. This is precisely why, when I fall down, I don't have to start from scratch with a plan B as I presumed. I don't even need a plan B. That's only what I thought I needed in order to bring closure to my failures and give me a place for a fresh start.

What I've found instead is that my pain, challenges, and personal failures add depth and growth to the plan He already has in place for me. The thing I was so desperate for when my perfectly laid plans failed me was a new plan, something concrete I could cling to. Turns out, all I really needed was to embrace the mystery of faith, not cling tightly to more plans. God already knew the plans and provision He had for my life:

I have it all planned out—plans to take care of you, not abandon you, plans to give you the future you hope for. When you call on Me, when you come and pray to Me, I'll listen. When you come looking for Me, you'll find me. Yes, when you get serious about finding Me and want it more than anything else, I'll make sure you won't be disappointed...I'll turn things around for you.[viii]

I don't need a plan B—ever. I just need to be open and curious to God's plans and provisions. I don't need do-overs or restarts. I only need to acknowledge my mistakes and accept failure as part of the journey. They are not interruptions or detours. Though painful, failure and disappointments are the rich, fertile valleys I walk. They challenge me to create space for honesty and acceptance. I'm not afraid or ashamed of imperfection anymore. It's exactly where I find authenticity...and God.

Endnotes

[i] Dr. Kevin Leman, *The Birth Order Book* (Grand Rapids: Revell, 2009), 80

[ii] Jeremiah 29:11, MSG

[iii] Gretchen Rubin, *Happiness Project* (New York: Harper Collins, 2009), 60

[iv] Psalm 56:8, MSG

[v] Psalm 42:1, paraphrased

[vi] Jeremiah 29:11, paraphrased

[vii] Psalm 3:3, paraphrased

[viii] Jeremiah 29:11-14, MSG

About the Author

Andria Flores spent over three decades of her life in pursuit of perfection, from straight As and gold stars, to marriage, babies, and a career. She dedicated herself to pleasing others in an attempt to earn love and approval—even from God. But in her late thirties, it became apparent that while perfectionism may have helped her achieve many of her life goals, it was not sustainable, not relatable, and not veritable.

Her subsequent unraveling led her to discover her authentic self, find vulnerability in relationships, and live life on her own terms with dreams and goals of her own choosing. Shedding the rigidity of perfectionism and people-pleasing has helped Andria wholly accept herself, develop and deepen her relationship with God, appreciate all the quirks and imperfections in her children, and find freedom and grace in love.

Contributors

Roger Leslie

Roger Leslie, prolific author and owner of Paradise Publishing, felt destined to be an author at age 13. Since then, he has followed a spiritual path filled with "fateful detours". That circuitous author's journey has included being a teacher, librarian, professor, book reviewer, writing coach, editor, and publisher. Each tangent, immersed in books, has accelerated the attainment of his overarching goal: to be a prolific author whose works inspire people to live the life they dream and empower them to discover God in their own way.
roger@paradisepublishing.com

Jen Aiken

Jen Aiken is a graphic designer who works with her clients on a wide variety of projects, including logo design, books, flyers, brochures, social media graphics, and billboards. She works alongside her clients, focusing on their goals and vision, to create ideal design solutions.
jen@jvodesign.com

Chris and Zhi Cook

Christopher & Zhivonni Cook are accomplished speakers and serve as public information officers for major law enforcement agencies in North Texas. When not engaged at their primary jobs, they also have a passion for photography and are members of the Professional Photographers of America and Texas Professional Photographers Association. They have won photo awards and had their photography featured in the Wall Street Journal, Maui 2020 annual calendar, and numerous policing journals. They capture special moments that last a lifetime.   .
PushingTheLens.com

Made in the USA
Coppell, TX
15 September 2020

38050464R00108